SALES LETTERS
READY TO GO!

Eleanor Dugan
William Bethel,
Consulting Editor

NTC Business Books
NTC/Contemporary Publishing Group

Library of Congress Cataloging-in-Publication Data

Dugan, Eleanor.
    Sales letters ready to go / Eleanor Dugan, William Bethel,
consulting editor.
        p.   cm.
    ISBN 0-8442-3566-0
    1. Sales letters—Handbooks, manuals, etc.   I. Bethel
William.   II. Title.
HF5730.D84   1995
    658.8'1—dc20   94-42410
                                                                CIP

ACKNOWLEDGMENTS

We wish to thank the following people for their invaluable contributions: Rick Barrera; Ann Bloch and *Writing Workout*; Lee Boyen; Marc Chapdelaine; René Chlumecky; Alan Cimberg; Jill Robin Coogan; Jim Courtney; John Jay Daly; Tom Dashiell; Steven P. Duddy of Coherent, Inc.; Joe Taylor Ford, editor/publisher of The Executive Speechwriter Newsletter; Ernest Gonzalez; Grizzard—the Direct Marketing Agency; Stu Heineckie; Kris Kmieciak; Sheila Murray Bethel; Sandy Nathan; Susan Neal; Nordic Track; Marianna Nunes; Laura Oden of EcoCartridge; Ray Pelletier; Jeff Powell; Joe Sabah; John Springer; Margot Summers; Dottie Walters; and Debbie Wright.

Published by NTC Business Books
A division of NTC/Contemporary Publishing Group, Inc.
4255 West Touhy Avenue, Lincolnwood (Chicago), Illinois 60646-1975 U.S.A.
Printed in the United States of America
International Standard Book Number: 0-8442-3566-0
    18   17   16   15   14   13   12   11   10   9   8   7   6   5   4   3

CONTENTS

1
What Is a Sales Letter?

Every letter that goes out over your signature is a potential "sales letter." It has the power to sell or sabotage, to lift you up or shoot you down.

You want your letters to represent you and what you sell with maximum impact, but few people can find the time to craft and polish every letter they send, to produce forceful and articulate letters day in and day out while excelling at all the other highly demanding aspects of sales.

That's why *Sales Letters Ready to Go* exists. It's designed to make your letter writing faster, easier, *and* more effective. You'll find examples of clear, powerful, persuasive letters, along with instructions for customizing them for every type of client and every stage of marketing, from your first prospecting letter to the messages that maintain the selling relationship over the years. These examples are drawn and adapted from Bill Bethel's forty years of successful selling and Eleanor Dugan's twelve years of creating original Executive Writing workbooks for Fortune 500 companies. Many of these letters have been contributed by some of the top people in sales.

WHAT ARE THE PITFALLS OF WRITING?

A good sales letter makes money. A poor sales letter loses money. It can cost you cold hard cash for wasted time, paper, and postage. It can cost you orders and business opportunities when it fails to develop new customers or persuade old ones. It can even cost you by having a negative effect on the reader: "I'll never do business with you bozos again, I'm withdrawing my account, canceling my order, and I'm going to tell anyone who'll listen what jerks you are!"

Obviously creating and sending any sales letter has so many potential pitfalls that many sensible people forget they are simply communicating on paper. They either go into hyper-drive, blasting readers with flamboyant ballyhoo reminiscent of a traveling medicine show, or they go to the other extreme in the mistaken belief that dignity lies in being bland and that decorum requires being indirect. Sometimes readers must struggle through several pages of ponderous prose before they can discover why the writer is writing (assuming the readers are still reading).

Having seen so many examples of ineffective sales letters, it's no wonder that some very successful people have decided, consciously or unconsciously, to stick to what they do best—selling—and to avoid the discomfort of being connected to weak, unsuccessful letters. They don't see strong sales letters as an essential facet of their total selling career.

WHAT IF YOU JUST DON'T WRITE?

Some people are so busy, so on the run, or so intimidated by the challenge of producing effective letters that they try to avoid letter writing altogether.

Here's the bad news: the letter that *should* be sent but isn't can be just as costly as a weak, hasty, or misguided message.

The good news is that today it's much easier to keep on top of correspondence through the magic of customized form letters, lap top computers, dictaphones, and tape recorders that work in the car, on planes, or in the shower. Good sales letters don't have to be time-intensive, and they don't have to be expensive. You can even gain good will and positive responses with a ten cent "tickler" card and three written words: "Great!" followed by your signature. (Make that two words if you only sign your first name.)

Remember:

Writing is not something you do in addition to selling.

*Writing **IS** selling.*

2
The Basic Sales Letter

Although we're going to be talking about a wide variety of "selling" letters in this book, the classic sales letter is a *prospecting* letter. It goes to a cold or almost-cold contact.

In a true cold-contact prospecting letter, you're trying to persuade a complete stranger to buy what you're selling. Often you're literally prospecting, sifting through a lot of useless gravel (people who don't want, don't need, or can't afford what you're selling) to find that one bright nugget of gold (a customer).

In a warmer version, your readers already have some affinity with you or with what you are selling. They may be current or past customers, or owners of the product for which you are offering accessories, or members of a group with strong interests in your services, or perhaps they live near your facility.

Letters to both cold and warm contacts start with your asking yourself the same six questions. Remember high school journalism class? That's where you were first introduced to the classic ingredients for reaching people on the printed page, the *Five W's and Sometimes H*: Who did What, When, Where, Why, and sometimes How. Though times may have changed, the *Five W's and Sometimes H* checklist is just as valuable today as it was for Ben Franklin, Horace Greeley, and Joseph Pulitzer.

THE WRITER'S SIX QUESTIONS

Before you write a sales letter, you should know the answers to these six crucial questions, the *Five W's and Sometimes H* :

> **Who** do you hope will make something happen?
> **What** exactly do you want to happen?
> **When** do you need or want results? In days? Weeks? Years?
> **Where** are these people? Or "*where* are they coming from?"
> **Why** a letter, instead of an ad, a phone call, or a visit?
> **How** *exactly* will it help to bring about the desired results?

Who? Decide exactly whom you're trying to reach. Who will be reading your letter? This "Who?" can be your entire mailing list or the one person in the XYZ company who can decide to do business with you.

What? Decide on your immediate and long-term goals. Do you want the reader to order a specific product or service directly, fill out a coupon for more information, agree to a meeting, sign up to attend an event, or simply have a positive feeling about you and what you are selling? Keep your objectives firmly in mind, and check your finished letter to be sure you've met them. It's okay to have both a short-term and long-term goal, but don't try to achieve too many things at once. You'll confuse your reader, diffuse your impact, and end up accomplishing little or nothing.

When? Decide "When" you need or want results. Is there a strong reason for emphasizing a quick response? Or are you investing in building trust and nurturing a selling relationship for the future? You must be clear in your own mind so you can convey this to the reader.

Where? The demographics of your potential customers and the intelligent use of mailing lists are both subjects for some research, thought, and ingenuity on your part. Be willing to do your homework.

If you're compiling lists of potential customers, you don't necessarily have to purchase expensive commercial lists. Your local library may have the information you need. Thousands of national and local directories are published every year. There are business directories like *Dunn & Bradstreet*, *Who's Who in Commerce & Industry*, and *Poor's Register of Directors & Executives*; industry directories like *Directory of American Automobile Dealers*, *Lockwood's Directory of Paper & Allied Trades*, *Insurance Almanac*, *Almanac of Realtors*, etc.; general directories like *National Social Directory*, *Who's Who in America*, and *American Architects Directory*; and many local phone directories and trade publications.

Why? Is a letter really the best way to reach this customer? Would a print or TV or radio ad be more efficient? Would voice mail or a colorful and informative flyer be more effective? The chief advantage of a letter is that you are fairly sure that your message will reach a particular person and be noticed, if only with annoyance as it is dropped unopened in the trash. But letters are expensive. Many of the current business letter books are updated versions of texts from the days when postage stamps cost 4¢ and secretaries made $25 a week. A first-class letter today costs a minimum of $2 and often several times that for postage, paper, envelope, time, equipment, and general overhead. So, why a letter? Why *this* letter?

How? How will this letter produce the results you want? What characteristics does it need to have to achieve this outcome? Create a mental scenario of what will change in the lives of the readers after they have read the letter and how your letter brought this about.

Of course, you don't have fill out a formal questionnaire every time you sit down to write a sales letter. After you've gotten used to using this valuable mental check list, it will become automatic, available to you whenever you are uncertain about how to proceed (or unsure why a particular letter didn't work as well as you had hoped). Once you know the answers to these six writer's questions, you are ready to connect with your reader.

THE READER'S SIX QUESTIONS

Each of your readers approaches your letter asking the same *Five W's and Sometimes H* questions you did, but in a slightly different order and from a very different point of view:

> **Who** is writing to me?
> **Why** should I bother to read this letter?
> **What** is someone trying to sell me?
> **How** will this product or service help me?
> **When** do I need to decide?
> **Where** can I get it?

Who *is writing me?* The name on your letterhead or your signature, if it is already familiar to the reader, may answer this question. If not, you should explain fairly early in your letter, for example:

> Now, you can experience the same superb quality and durability in your home that has made Allied the state's leading luxury hotel supplier for fifteen years.
>
> •   •   •
>
> We're new in Wisconsin and eager to show you why more than 10,000 Chicagoans have been loyal customers of our northern Illinois branches for the past three years.
>
> •   •   •
>
> Until now, you had to be in Finland to sleep under a legendary, handwoven Kotka reindeer-hair blanket. Starting Monday, we'll save you the $1100 airfare.

Why *should I bother to read this letter?* This question is usually answered by the opening paragraph, often called the "hook." It explains why you are writing and positions the reader for information that follows. In traditional cold-contact letters the hook is a clever or alarming statement intended to get the reader to keep reading. However, in today's busy, no-nonsense world, cute or pretentious openers are often one-way tickets to the wastebasket. A simple overview statement can be even more effective:

> Our product may be twice as good as the one you're using because ...

> Here are five ways our new service will help you to ...

> We can save you time, money, and grief if you ...

Respect the reader's time and intelligence. Get to the point.

What *is someone trying to sell me?* If you conceal your purpose until the bottom of page three, you'd better have a darn good reason because, chances are, your reader won't still be reading.

How *will this product or service help me?* Here's where you sell those *features* and *benefits*. See page 16.

When *do I need to decide?* This may be irrelevant, but it's important to point out any actual deadlines. If the reader needs to respond by a certain date, highlight that information, even move it up to the first paragraph. This *doesn't* mean turning a letter into a garish "L*A*S*T C*H*A*N*C*E — Going Out of Business" type poster. Instead, try some of the emphasizing techniques under *Highlighting* on page 48.

Where *can I get it?* Unless your purpose is to tantalize, to excite interest for something not yet available, or to build desire for a major future purchase, don't forget to spell out exactly where the reader can obtain the product or service. Provide an address, a phone number, an order form, a list of local distributors, etc. Don't lose that red-hot Impulse to Buy moment while the reader hunts for a way to respond. Make it easy!

A TYPICAL SALES LETTER

Here's how a characteristic prospecting letter would address the reader's *Five W's and Sometimes H.* Note that the *When* and *Where* are less important in this example, but they would be crucial to the message if you were announcing an event or a deadline.

WHO

The Bank of North Yonkers
111 Main Street
Yonkers, MI 53328

Dear

WHY
WHAT

Here's an outstanding credit card offer that may
dramatically cut the cost of your credit. How? It's easy.

IIOW

- You'll get an incredibly low Annual Percentage
  Rate of only 9.9%. The rates of most other cards
  are 3% to 7% higher.

- There's no annual fee.

- You'll also get free extra cards, an immediate
  $500 cash advance at your request, and more!

The bottom line? Over the life of your card, you may save
hundreds — even thousands — of dollars on fees and
finance charges.

HOW

So, if you're ready to switch to a credit card that could
lower your payments, month after month, just fill out the

WHEN

application below and send it to me today.

Sincerely,

WHO

Jess Lasorda
Credit Co-ordinator

WHERE

ENCL: Reply card

WHAT YOU ARE REALLY SELLING?

No matter what you are trying to sell, every human being you'll ever meet is buying just one thing: *hope*. Hope motivates every transaction. Each morning we get up, hoping that today is the day when something is going to be better. Your readers want to believe that someone somewhere is going to solve their problems, relieve their stress, and increase their comfort and pleasure. Is that person you? Tell them how!

3
The Six Steps
to Great Sales Letters

You've learned the six questions to ask yourself before you write and the six questions your readers will ask when they open your letters. Now that you're ready to sit down and write, let's look at the *Six Steps to Great Sales Letters*:

Step 1. Decide on your purpose.
Step 2. Picture your customer.
Step 3. Decide what you are *really* selling.
Step 4. Create a strong opening.
Step 5. Overcome potential objections.
Step 6. Make your letters easy to read.

STEP 1. DECIDE ON YOUR PURPOSE

Obviously the purpose of a sales letter is to sell. But who, what, when, where, why, and how? An amazing number of missives are sent out without definite goals. Some routine sales letters are even enough off-target to be counter-productive.

You are about to write your letter. Ask these questions:

• What do you want to be different after you send this letter? Describe— jot your response on a note pad if necessary—and evaluate. For example, do you want your reader:

> TO ACT - To do something specific right now, such as return a coupon, send a check, come to an event, or grant an interview.

TO FEEL - To like and trust you, your product, or your service, now and in the future.

TO LEARN - To acquire information that will enable them to make more intelligent choices in the future. (Thus, perhaps, saving you time and energy while making you their consultant and ally.)

• Are you trying to expand your user base? Increase orders from current customers? Refine or redefine your client list?

• Is the purpose of the letter to maintain the status quo? To keep a relationship, image, or market niche from eroding?

• How important is it to promote the image and identity of your company? What qualities do you want to project? Energy, efficiency, prudence, daring, reliability, competence, knowledgeability, versatility, etc.?

• Are you trying to build an ongoing sales relationship or is this a one-time deal?

Stand-Alone Letters

Some products and services can "sell themselves" through a letter. The letter is the only connection with the customer before the reader responds by telephoning an order or mailing a check or turning up at a place or event.

Open-the-Door Letters

For other products and services, the letter is only the beginning. Its purpose is to arrange an interview or a demonstration or to urge the reader to request more in-depth information. For example, Bill Bethel, coauthor of this book, sells speeches, workshops, and sales training programs tailored to the needs of each client. Obviously, only a few managers hire him cold, never having met him or seen him in action. So Bill's cold prospecting letters include a request for an interview or phone conversation to discuss the client's needs. Bill also asks readers if they would like to see a demo tape. Such open-the-door letters usually start the sales process for high-priced items, once-in-a-lifetime purchases, and customized products and services.

Build-a-Relationship Letters

When a long-term association between customer and supplier is desirable or essential to the selling process, every letter doesn't have to push a particular product. Often what you are selling is a relationship: trust, esteem, rapport. You are making your company and yourself indispensable to the smooth functioning of your customers' business or personal lives. Such letters can offer relevant news and tips:

> I just heard that your firm will be opening a new facility near Detroit next spring. This might be a good opportunity for us to ...
>
> • • •
>
> How are the new regulations going to affect your Scranton plant? I've done some research for another client in your area, and I'd be glad to send you a copy ...

Clarify your goals, what you want your letter to do. Write these goals down if necessary, and check your first draft to be sure you are addressing them. Then let your readers know exactly what response you'd like.

STEP 2. PICTURE YOUR CUSTOMER

Imagine your readers are picking up your letter. Where are they? What else is competing for their attention? Did they get a lot of other mail that day? What will the other letters look like? Be about? How many seconds do you think you have to engage their interest before they go on to the next demand for their time? Will they even open the envelope? (Think about the amount of mail you drop unopened in the wastebasket!)

Are you more likely to succeed with your reader if your letter stands out as different? Or if it blends in, but is better written and organized? Should it be flashier or more conservative? More formal or more casual? Longer or shorter? Does the nature of your product and the setting in which the readers read lend itself to a leisurely once-upon-a-time story approach? Or is brevity essential? If your readers' mail is likely to be prescreened by assistants, what impact will your letter have on them and how can you get them on your side?

Is your reader the person you expect to respond? Or are others involved in the decision to buy? Do you hope your reader will be impressed and recommend you to others? How much time and energy do you want to invest in good will?

When you approach people in person, you get lots of signals about their receptivity to you and what you want to say: their basic body language and manner; how they are dressed; their surroundings; whether they seem alert, tired, happy, or grumpy; the situation you find them in; and what they are doing at the time. You can adjust your words and tone of voice, your facial expression, energy level, and where and how you stand to fit the situation. You know immediately if you start to lose their attention, and you can respond by varying your actions to control the rhythm of interaction.

But when you write, you are, in effect, shouting into the void. Most salespeople are "people-people," and they can find this really frustrating— like actors switching from live theater to filming on a hushed sound stage. Writing to an unseen reader requires the same conscious mental shift, a honing of the ability to visualize an invisible audience so you can speak with the same immediacy and intimacy that you do face to face.

- Who *precisely* is your audience? (Are you sure?)

- How do these people think? Process information? Are they likely to be slightly more receptive to verbal information? Or to visual information?

- What is the most important thing to them? (Forget *your* interests. Put yourself in your customers' place.)

- What motivates them, makes them tick?

- What are the events and mental processes of the reader that will bring this about?

- In what environment will your letter be read? What else may be competing for the reader's attention? How will you overcome this?

- What *exactly* do you want the reader to do after reading your letter? How are you going to encourage this?

Do your homework, whether you're writing to one or a thousand. Find out everything you can about these people, their priorities, problems, hopes, and fears. Role-play for a few moments. Step into your reader's skin.

People don't buy sunscreen, they buy protection from painful sunburn and skin cancer. They don't buy burglar alarms, they buy security and peace of mind. They don't buy VCRs, they buy pleasure and convenience. You are not selling things. You are selling ideas, concepts, feelings, self-image, and satisfaction.

Some buying motivations seem straightforward enough. Thirsty people buy beverages. Painters buy paint. But which beverages, which paint? Motivations are rarely simple. Decisions are influenced by cultural or environmental factors, by education, past experience, social status, income, and the opinions of friends, neighbors and family. All of these factors affect the strength of the buying motives and all vary from person to person and from time to time.

Every human being abounds with complex needs. The number and kind depend upon temperament, education, lifestyle, and cultural expectations. Some needs create tension which must be alleviated. This tension converts a need to a desire. Not until this stage is reached is the prospect ready to buy. People will buy something they *want* before they will buy something they *need*!

As you scan the following list, consider what you know or can guess about your readers' "demographics"—age, sex, education, geographical location, income, occupation, hobbies, affinity groups, marital status, children, etc.—anything that might be relevant to their feelings about your product.

Psychologists have confirmed that all well-adjusted people see themselves as slightly better than they actually are. Without this mild and useful megalomania, few of us would bother to get out of bed in the morning. Write to your readers both as they are and as they want to be.

How do they want to see themselves? In their slightly idealized self-image, are they:

respected leader	competent
hard bargainer	compassionate
wise counselor	shrewd judge
good person	foresighted

level-headed business person	generous
patriotic	thrifty
competitive	sophisticated
rebel	helpless victim
conformist	outraged victim
expansive liberal	sympathetic ally
cautious conservative	unique, a standout
trendsetter	one of a group
trend follower	out of the mainstream

Do they have hopes, fears, and concerns about:

Being in control
Being safe (from what?)
Being liked/loved
Being sought after
Being left alone

To fulfill these hopes and conquer these fears, do they want:

To be better looking (That is, to conform to whatever the
       current image of attractiveness is.)
To be richer (Why? To achieve more status, control, or comfort?)
Less stress and discomfort
More pleasure
More status
More sense of control
To be healthier (as long as it doesn't conflict with pleasure or
       "looking good")
To make loved ones happier or healthier
A better community
World peace

Is it their priority to avoid:

Hassles and inconvenience
Disapproval
Embarrassment
Stress or distress

Uncertainty, ambiguity
Fear
Pain
Danger

What social issues are important to them?
What do they hate?
What do they love?
What or whom do they want to feel superior to?
What intimidates them?
What bores them?

Does wishful thinking, hypocrisy, or plain old human nature create a gap between what they say they want and what they actually want? Human beings are notorious for giving lip service to ideals and then doing otherwise. How much "fudge factor" do you need to allow?

Now do you now have a better picture of the person you're talking to on paper?

What Does Your Customer Think of You?

A further part of *Step 2 - Picture your customer* is to decide how they regard and evaluate *you*. Turn your telescope around and imagine they are looking at you.

How do they see you and what you sell? Are you reliable, outmoded, on the cutting edge, risky, unresponsive, traditional, hot, too trendy, rare and precious, rare and too hard to find, hard to use, widely available and convenient, too widely available and ubiquitous? How does public perception line up with reality? (It can take several years for changes within an organization, good or bad, to be recognized by the general public.)

Do You Need to Change Your Image?

Is the reader's opinion of your product favorable? Or do you want to try to change it? Here are some strategies for using sales letters to change your image.

IF YOUR READERS PERCEIVE YOU AS:	TRY THIS:
Fuddy duddy, too conservative	Warmer, more casual tone
Too flaky	Conservative letterhead, formal tone
Uncaring	Prove awareness of readers' problems
Outdated	Stress that your extensive experience provides extra insight into new trends
Too hard to get	"We're worth the effort because ..."
Too slow	"We're worth the wait because ..."
Not as good as competitors	"But we do excel at ..."
Unreliable	Admit past mistakes, say why and how things will improve
Dishonest	Ditto!

Incorporate your image-changing strategies into your sales letters. They can even provide a talking point, a lever to create new interest in your product. You'll find more strategies for challenging customers' preconceptions and misconceptions on page 20.

STEP 3. DECIDE WHAT YOU ARE *REALLY* SELLING

Are you selling haircuts or self esteem? R-values or comfort? Germ-killing detergent or peace of mind? More copies per minute or more time for creative work and relaxation? The one thing you're probably *not* selling is your product or service. You're selling what it can do for the buyer.

Features, Benefits, and Motivations

Every product or service sells because of three things. Two you probably know about. "Features and Benefits" has been drummed into every salesperson's head over and over. To this classic selling mantra, you can add *motivation*.

- Features - What the product/service is.
- Benefits - What the product/service does.
- Motivation - Your answers to the customer's questions: "What's in it for me? How does this make my life better?" In other words, "So what?"

A simplification might be: Has → Does → Means

- Has - Features
- Does - Benefits
- Means - Motivation

For example, an employee relocation service:

- **Has** affiliations with 2,700 realtors, 20 moving companies, and 400 personal relocation counselors in 46 states and 20 foreign countries, plus reduced-price travel arrangements, computerized school searches, substantial discounts on furnishings for the new home, etc. (*Features*)

- **Does** provide fast, complete, one-stop relocation services for your employees and their families at a lower overall cost than if you contracted individually with the various services. Probably decreases employee stress and increases satisfaction, morale, and family support, thus providing greater productivity. (*Benefits*)

- **Means** you as an employer have greater flexibility in reassigning personnel, leading to a sense of power, control, and prestige. (*Motivations*)

Or a new electronic door lock:

- **Has** a sophisticated sound-analyzing computer chip.

- **Does** recognize authorized voices and responds to them.

- **Means** extra security against intruders, plus you'll never be locked out again if you forget or lose your key.

Sometimes a writer is trying to sell features to a reader who is only interested in benefits. Your job is to demonstrate that the *features* provide *benefits* that create powerful *motivations* to buy. If the connection isn't obvious, make it unmistakable. Prove that what you're selling is worth far more in satisfaction than what it will cost. Some benefits must be spelled out:

> • **Better Density.** Our cartridges measured a density of 1.4 compared to 1.29 for Standard's cartridge, using a densitometer. (A higher number means a darker image.)

Sometimes you can be pretty sure that the average reader will be able to infer benefits from the features:

> Enjoy many other advantages from the Allied Kredit Kard:
>
> • Acceptance at over 10 million locations
> • Access to over 120,000 automated teller machines (ATMs)
> • 24-hour customer service
> • 25-day grace period for purchases

Most readers will mentally translate these Kredit Kard features into personal benefits. But never assume that cost, functions, or speed will automatically transform into *cheaper*, *more convenient*, or *faster*. Don't even assume that *cheaper*, *more convenient*, or *faster* will be perceived as real benefits by a customer who may be more concerned about reliability, control, or status. You are responsible for creating the chain of associations:

> More copies per second means your staff will spend less time in the back room doing paperwork. They can be out on the floor where they belong, serving customers and making sales.
>
> • • •
>
> At Wellington we tan our own leathers, forge our own brasses, and hand-shape every inch of our custom saddles. That's why their durability, style, and comfort are legendary. A Wellington saddle has graced the back of every regional champion for the last thirteen years, and each of those saddles is still a prized possession of its prize-winning owner.

You can reverse the order and put the "so what?" first:

> You'll never wash another window. The Sonic-Scrub makes messy buckets and squeegees obsolete. No more climbing ladders or balancing on windowsills. No more brushes, rags, or smelly solvents. Just pass the unique Laser-Wand over any window, open or closed. Grit, film, and dirt vibrate loose in seconds, leaving the glass cleaner than when it left the factory. **Sonic-Scrub DOES windows!**

The emotional appeal of each of these products—having more control over employees' time, associating with champions, eliminating a nasty job everyone hates—represents your speculations about your readers' motivations, your answer to their unspoken "so what?"

What's Your Real News?

When you're trying to see yourself and your product from your potential customer's point of view, ask yourself: "What's the real news?" What is the most important thing you are offering? Does your letter convey this?

One classic missed-opportunity letter is a three page gem from a computer consulting firm. The first two pages tell the reader that the company has recently merged with another similar company. Then there is a list of the computers the firm can now support, the products it now offers, and the extensive training of its enlarged staff. Way down near the bottom of page three is a casual mention that, because of the merger, the firm can now offer emergency service twenty-four hours a day, seven days a week!

If you were a prospective customer, what was the most important news in this letter? If you had done business in the past, you might have checked whether the phone number or address had changed, but probably you wouldn't have cared much about the merger itself. As you waded through the fifteen or so paragraphs—if you did—most likely you would have begun muttering: "What's in it for me?" Obviously having skilled consultants, a larger selection, and lower prices are all pleasant benefits, but the one thing with overwhelming appeal to anyone who has ever had a computer crash in the middle of an important job is the 24-hour service! That one benefit, tucked so shyly at the end of the letter, should have been in red on the letterhead and in the first sentence of the letter.

Re-evaluate your list of features and benefits from your potential customers' point of view. What would *they* find most appealing? Are you stressing the right thing?

"What's in It for Me?"

When you can answer this question vividly and truthfully, you've probably made the sale. An easy way to tie the characteristics of what you're selling to your prospects' wants and needs is Bill Bethel's *So/Because Rule*. If you start by writing about a feature, continue with "so ... " Then show how that feature produces a benefit. If you start with the benefit, follow it with "because ... " and specify the feature:

(name feature) *so* ... (describe benefit)
(describe benefit) *because* ... (name feature)

It doesn't matter which way you do it:

We've eliminated 90% of the paperwork *so* you can process your claim in less than five minutes.

or:

You can process your claim in less than five minutes *because* we've eliminated 90% of the paperwork.

Benefits may or may not be motivations in themselves. If the motivation for experiencing a specific benefit won't be overwhelmingly obvious in the mind of the reader, spell it out.

Zero-in on Motivations

Put your hunches and solid research about your prospects' motivations to work when you craft your sales letter. Push their motivational buttons. Here are some examples of addressing different motivations.

Motivations: Status, control, financial safety: Here's a good letter to busy young lawyers that addresses some of their frequent concerns and strong motivations.

State Bar Association
Membership Benefits Committee

Dear (Bar Member):

Your plea for a quick and simple insurance application process has been heard!

Do you have a new job, child, or house?. Then you know that just when you have the least spare time, it's more important than ever to be on top of the changes in your financial responsibilities.

We understand and we've made it possible for you to get full information on the different levels of our Group Term Plan — all at affordable group rates! Just take two minutes to fill out the enclosed card and drop it in the mail. We'll get back to you within a week with a full written recommendation. <u>No strings</u>. No obligations.

Lawyers want to be seen as competent and in control in a fast-paced environment, but, like the cobbler whose children go barefoot, lawyers often can't or don't take the time to handle their own affairs properly. This letter starts by acknowledging the readers' importance and then offers a guilt-free, labor-free panacea for a common niggling discomfort. And it's short!

Motivations: Economy, Social Conscience: An attention-getting letterhead and the double message of saving money and the environment make this real letter a powerful motivator.

EcoCartridge®
Cartridge Recycling & Printer Service

P.O. Box 2582
Merrifield, VA 22116
Tel: 202/483-1200

Dear

Finally, EcoCartridge has proof that our cartridges are better than Hewlett Packard's. In an independent laboratory test, EcoCartridge's recycled toner cartridges outperformed Hewlett Packard's <u>new</u> cartridges in every single test.

• **More Prints.** Our cartridge yielded 1506 acceptable printed pages compared to a Hewlett Packard cartridge which produced only 969 printed pages. (All testing used the internal HP Series II "04" test pattern.)

• **Less Toner.** The amount of toner required to print a single page with the "04" test pattern was .0161162019 grams, compared to Hewlett Packard's .28895769 grams.

• **Better Density.** Our cartridges measured a density of 1.4 compared to 1.29 for Hewlett Packard's cartridge using a densitometer. (A higher number means a darker image.)

• **More rugged.** Our cartridges passed all Shipping and Image Tests. They were subjected to both air travel and UPS delivery and passed all seal quality tests.

EcoCartridges save your money. You'll save over 50% if you're still buying new cartridges. We have established a reputation for providing the highest quality recycled toner cartridges available for laser printers, along with personalized service.

EcoCartridges save your planet. You'll feel better about buying a recycled product without any sacrifice in quality. Our remanufacturing process starts with choosing only the best used parts from empty cartridges and then supplementing them with new parts. We recondition all drums, wiper blades, and magnetic rollers, then use rigorous testing to guarantee your complete satisfaction.

EcoCartridge is a solely woman-owned business with experience in both private industry and government agencies. I personally ensure quality at every level and keep in close contact with every client. I know if and when a problem occurs and see that appropriate steps are taken immediately.

We look forward to doing business with you in this new year!

Sincerely,

Laura Oden
Owner, EcoCartridge

Encl: Printer list

(Used with permission of author)

Ms. Oden says, "This was the beginning of the most successful direct mail campaign I ever did, resulting in twenty new clients within sixty days — very good for us."

Motivations: Status, Power, Approval, Political Correctness: Few things are more nerve-wracking than having to make decisions that can backfire through no fault of your own. This is a common dilemma in areas with a high human factor such as personnel, marketing, training, and production design. Here's a letter that Sheila Murray Bethel sends out to people responsible for booking speakers for conventions and seminars. (Imagine the feedback and impact on your career if the expensive speaker you've chosen has 4,000 people squirming in their seats. And imagine the advantages of booking a hit.)

> Dear
>
> Wouldn't it be stimulating to give your members a speaker with a clear, insightful, action-provoking, and entertaining message?
>
> Wouldn't it be helpful to present a speaker who has both a national and global reputation and perspective?
>
> Wouldn't it be great if the speaker has a book on the topic of leadership (90,000 copies sold to date), and was invited by the ASAE Foundation to write a monograph for *Association Leadership in the 21st Century*?
>
> AND wouldn't it be refreshing if the speaker just happens to be female?
>
> Sincerely,
>
> Sheila Murray Bethel

(Used with permission of author)

STEP 4. CREATE A STRONG OPENING

This doesn't mean "cute" or bizarre. The humor columns are full of overwritten opening sentences that fell flat, "Letters I Never Finished Reading ..." Starting letters with jokes, old sayings, famous quotes, or self-serving questions—the standbys of 1930s—just doesn't work today.

Dated:

You never know what's going to happen, do you? One man we know had to close his flea circus because his star ran off with a poodle.

•   •   •

Artemus Ward said, "It ain't what you know that'll hurt you. It's what you know that ain't so."

•   •   •

The other day a friend asked us how we can serve so many customers and still keep them all happy.

Boring:

The foremost responsibility of Executive Management is to define the mission and chart the overall course and direction for the company. (*So what?*)

•   •   •

We pharmacists can never know enough about the newest drugs, can we? (*Speak for yourself.*)

•   •   •

Just a little note to say "hello," and to let you know what's happening at Allied. (*You mistake me for someone who cares.*)

Irritating:

Have you ever looked in the mirror and asked yourself ... (*No!*)
No longer need haste make waste. (*Yawn.*)
This may be your last chance to ... (*Promise?*)

Inappropriate:

During the war I spent sixteen days on the front lines, without food or water, pinned down by withering enemy fire. That's why I appreciate what it is like for you members of the Northern State Used Car Association to be on the "front lines" of selling.

Better:

> Can you *talk* your people into greater productivity, loyalty, or motivation? Frequently.
>
> •   •   •
>
> If your firm has new hires, interns, or business associates coming to the Denver area, we can save you <u>half</u> the cost of the average hotel room.
>
> •   •   •
>
> Your monthly rent check can cover a $158,000 + home loan.

A strong opening grabs attention honestly and positions the reader for what follows.

Tell the Reader Why You are Writing

In today's busy world, if your letter is lucky enough to pass the Shall-I-open-this? test, you have three to five seconds to position yourself. If you fail, your letter goes straight into the round filing cabinet. You have 50 words tops—maybe only 10—to tell readers exactly why you are writing and why they should keep reading.

Here's another 100% real letter, typos and all, disguised because it is an example of what *not* to do. Imagine that you are a busy executive who is also active in professional organizations and community service. How long does it take you to figure out why the writer is writing?

☑   Put a check in the margin when you finally figure out the writer's purpose, and underline the sentence that spells it out.

Try to guess why this writer is writing:

Professional Fund Raising Consultants
P.O. Box 2222
Greeneville, WI 99999

```
Dear

      I would like to take this opportunity to
introduce myself and the companies that I represent.
This is my sixteenth year in the fund raising business
```

Why is this writer writing? - continued

and I take a great deal of pride in the variety of items I have available as well as the dependable service I have provided over the years. As I travel throughout the state, I find that the same problem exists irregardless of the size of the school: NOT ENOUGH MONEY! I would appreciate your looking over the information below which gives you a basic idea of the companies I deal with and the types of items available. I feel confident that there is one (or a combination) that would meet your needs and adapt to the economy of your area.

HAPPY ORCHARD FARMS: The largest catalog-type fundraising company in the state. They provide a wide variety of items at a variety of prices. The catalogues are geared to Christmas, Easter, or a year round is available as well. Having just gotten back from the Happy Orchard Farms annual meeting, I again have seen the excellent quality, fair pricing, and high profits schools across the country attain using Happy Orchard Farms.

SWEETIES COMPANY: They are the makers of such fine candies as Bozos, Big-Bites, Sweetums, and Goof-balls. The candies taste wonderful and our programs are geared to fit your needs. Excellent profit margin too!

JERK MASTER: Maker of high quality beef sticks and jerky which is distributed nation-wide. Many of my schools use this as an alternative to candy sales with excellent results or possibly you would like a combination of both.

GLOO-YOU's: This is truly the most interested fundraising company to come along since I used to sell Fat the Cat! Gloo-loo's, founded by Jack Jackson, the creator and owner of Bogo-Pogo, is a new and exciting program. The plastic decals cling like magic to any glossy surface and are reusable year after year.

Why is this writer writing? - continued

Affordable, cute, educational, and different, these items are year round family fund and because of the additionals of new designs, a traditional fundraiser for your group!

INVENT-AN-IMAGE: The most interesting T-shirt I have ever seen! You can choose up to ten activity designs which depict your school and school's activities. You can include your school name, a detailed drawing of the front of your school, and the activity designs which you provide. The five color graphics on white backing make a most descriptive T-shirt. A one of a kind KEEPSAKE!

All of the above are wonderful programs, but you would know your area and your needs best. I would appreciate hearing from you to set up a meeting with your board. In addition I would gladly provide you with references if you should so request.

Sincerely,

(Note that all errors are verbatim from the original letter! "Fund raising" is alternately spelled as one and two words, punctuation is casual, and two different spellings of the word "catalogue" occur in the same paragraph. If you want to impress, proofread, proofread, proofread!)

You're right! The writer *never* says, "I handle an exciting line of wholesale fundraising items that students can easily resell to raise money for their schools." The reader is forced to infer this. The first clue is "Fund Raising" in the letterhead. Then the writer talks about "items available" and "dependable service." He then mentions "schools" and "money." A truly dedicated reader can guess the purpose of the letter at about this point, but few busy people have the time and energy for this kind of effort.

So, even though you may know exactly why you are writing, do your readers the courtesy of letting them in on the secret. Put your purpose in the first paragraph.

The Perfect First Paragraph

Your ideal opening has two qualities:

1. It tells the reader why you are writing.
2. It persuades the reader to keep reading.

Here are some examples:

> Because your firm is a member of the State Trade Association, you are entitled to a one-time 30% discount on our newest FAX models plus a generous allowance for your old FAX machine. This means it is actually <u>less expensive</u> to upgrade to a plain paper FAX than to continue using your present machine.
>
> • • •
>
> If you fly with Allied Airlines and bank with First Allied Bank, you can accumulate Bonus Flyer Miles even faster.
>
> • • •
>
> When you do business in a foreign country, you need to keep up with that country's changing tax laws. The **Annual International Tax Directory** makes sure you do.
>
> • • •
>
> We've heard that your firm is considering a move to the Bay Area. Because we've helped more than 400 out-of-state firms relocate here with a minimum of disruption and expense, we'd like the opportunity to tell you how we did it and show you what we can do for you.
>
> • • •
>
> Call us the next time you have a crushing deadline and need exceptional service. We're the Emergency Experts and we <u>love</u> a challenge. If it's impossible, we do it anyway!
>
> • • •
>
> We're different from any cleaning service you've ever used and we'd like to show you why.
>
> • • •
>
> Before you pay full price for roses, please let us give you a quote. Don't be intimidated by our (well-deserved) reputation for superb quality and service. Because we have exclusive access to the most productive and innovative growers in the area, we can offer you exquisite blooms at more than competitive prices.

Prove you appreciate your readers' time and attention by getting to the point, even if this means losing them. When you're prospecting, you're trying to separate people who'll buy what you've got from people who won't. If readers discard your letter after the first paragraph because they don't want your product, don't need it, or can't afford it, that's okay. They've disqualified themselves, allowing you to focus on your real prospects. They've also been made aware of what you sell, and they haven't been inconvenienced. If you didn't make a sale, you may have generated some name recognition that will lead to a future sale.

STEP 5. OVERCOME POTENTIAL OBJECTIONS

In person, every good salesperson is trained to overcome objections, to use them as valuable leverage for greater communication and an ultimate sale. When you write a sales letter, you can't have that valuable interchange, so you have to anticipate objections.

Some Common Objections

Imagine yourself standing in your readers' shoes. Try to imagine all the reasons they might reject you. Then address those issues head-on in the introduction or body of your letter.

"I don't want it." Point out benefits they may not have considered.

> Here are six ugly jobs you'll <u>never</u> have to do again if you decide to invest in an Allied compactor.
>
> • • •
>
> You've never used an outside contractor before. It's a brand new idea for you, I know, but our current clients tell us that we save them an average of 100 hours a month <u>and</u> we cost less than if they did the job in-house. Here's how: (and continue with a bulleted list)

"I don't need it." Stress benefits.

> Who needs a Super-Surge Protector? Just people with computer files they'd rather not lose.

• • •

No one <u>needs</u> a goosedown pillow. But our customers swear they couldn't live without one.

• • •

Your FAX system works 95% of the time. Is that good enough?

"I can't afford it."

Can you afford it? Updating your system may offer a payback in as little as 13 months. That means it's actually <u>cheaper</u> to install Allied than to continue as you are. May I show you how?

• • •

I recognize that this is a big decision, but if I can show you how you can afford it and stay on budget, would that solve your problem with ...?

• • •

Yes, their equipment is cheaper, but ours lasts longer. That means you'll enjoy a faster, more reliable system that costs you <u>less</u> per month for the pleasure of using it.

	Initial cost	Life span	Cost/month
Theirs	$33,540.	48 months average*	$698.75
Ours	$45,200.	80 months guaranteed**	$565.00

*   Survey of owners, published in June, 1999 *Industry Report*
**   GUARANTEED by our maintenance policy!

"I prefer another product/service."

Yes, our competitor has an outstanding record and has been around a long time. That's why we've concentrated on the kind of individual service and customized attention that a big company like that just can't offer.

• • •

You've had a long and successful relationship with Consolidated, and we hope they'll continue to provide for your needs for a long time to come. But right now Allied is offering some unique supports and features that Consolidated hasn't thought about yet. For example, we can: (continue with bulleted list)

"Not now ..."

> Of course, you're going to want to think this over and talk it over. When you do, remember these key points: (continue with bulleted list)
>
> •   •   •
>
> What's going to be different six months from now if you don't decide? And what's going to be different if you <u>do</u>?

Turn Negatives Into Positives

What's the worst thing that your competitors could say about you? What's the absolutely worst thing your potential customers could think about you? Confront the objection head on. Nip it in the bud.

"You're too hard to find."

> *Angelo's* is Washington's best kept secret. Woodward and Bernstein have never found it. Power lunchers don't know it exists, and we want to keep it that way—our handmade pastas and secret-recipe sauces aren't for the masses. In fact, unless you knew we were here, you'd probably pass right by our green front door. That's why we're enclosing a map ...
>
> •   •   •
>
> A lot of people just give up when they can't find Orgo-Farms nut butters at their local health food store. They don't have the time and energy to track us down, so they settle for another brand, one that's almost as good.
>
> We hate that. We never settle for second best, so why should you? That's why we're now offering our scrumptious line of nut butters by mail ...

"Your deliveries aren't reliable."

> <u>Why some orders have been late</u>: The amazing success of the *Mr. Asteroid* star viewers took us by surprise. We knew this was going to be a hot seller, but your response has been overwhelming! We're enormously grateful, and we're working

day and night to meet current orders. We anticipate being back on schedule by March 1st. In the meantime ...

●   ●   ●

You've been inconvenienced — and we've been tearing our hair out because too many of our past shipments arrived late. <u>No one should have to go through that</u>! We think we've solved the problem, and just in time, while we still have some hair left. Starting September 5th ...

"It's too hard to use."

If the Allied System were simple enough for anyone to operate, it would be too simple to do the job! We know you need the power and versatility of an Allied System, but you <u>don't</u> need any headaches or lost time. That's why we include full training and support services for the first six months.

●   ●   ●

<u>Don't panic</u>. At first glance, operating the HomeLion Security System can seem as overwhelming as flying a 747. But—just like learning to tie your shoes—after a few tries, the process becomes completely automatic. Our patient and nurturing consultant will walk you through arming and disarming the system until you are completely comfortable with the process.

Even if you're not face to face with your customers, you can anticipate their objections. Then shoot down the "Yes, but ..." before it shoots *you* down.

STEP 6. MAKE YOUR LETTERS EASY TO READ

With most sales letters, you've got just a few seconds to grab or lose the reader. The overall look of your letter and the ease with which the reader can scan it can win you the time you need to make your connection.

A fine letter is like a fine painting. The eye can dance down the page, previewing and grasping the contents, then go back for a careful examination. Visual appeal is essential. Organize information in your letter so your reader can preview in the same way. Here are some guidelines—rules, if you will—that can help.

Why Rules?

Everyone hopes to find a secret formula, a set of rules that will guarantee a positive reaction to every sales letter every time. But remember: rules are always created after the fact. Something is terrific or awful, so people go back and try to decide why it worked or didn't work. Then they formulate some guidelines for reproducing the success factor and avoiding failure. This works fairly well—most of the time—in art, in sales letter writing, even in choosing a mate. But it can never take every variable into consideration.

Occasionally, an extraordinarily successful sales letter defies all logic based on past experience. That's why you may look at some experts' BEFORE and AFTER examples with genuine amazement, finding you much prefer the original version: "That's exactly how *I* talk and it's always worked for *me*."

So, the most important rule for great sales letters is that—occasionally—it is okay to break all the so-called rules if you are 100% confident about your potential customers and how they will respond. A long, chatty, get-to-the-point-on-page-3 letter that would fail utterly in a high-pressure environment might be perfect for some of your clients. Or a brief, concise letter could be seen as brusque and insulting by a particular audience that demands a leisurely approach. A formal tone could be seen as stiff, old fashioned, or unfriendly; a casual tone as rude or presumptuous. To choose the best approach, you must truly know yourself, your product, and your customers.

Don't Write Like You Talk

Salespeople are famous for their strong verbal skills. So why do many of them hate to write? It's because the part of the brain that governs speech is different from the part that directs writing. That's the reason many excellent speakers would rather have a root canal than write a letter, while some world-famous writers are totally tongue-tied in public. (You can probably think of examples of both.)

Standard advice to hesitant writers is, "Write like you talk." But, spoken language just isn't written language. If you've ever seen a typed transcript of a dynamic, successful presentation or speech (maybe one of your own), you'll understand why. The presenter used body language, shifts in vocal color and emphasis, eye contact, facial expressions, gestures, and pauses to communicate. But on the printed page, the actual words seem flat and dull.

Or think of the reverse, the presenter who reads from a written page. Usually it sounds stilted and boring!

Moral: Written language is different from spoken language.

The trick to "writing like you talk" is to keep your writing lively and engaging — to convert the intent, energy, and pacing of the original spoken words into words that convey the same rhythms and impact on the printed page.

> **Tape transcript:** When you analyze all the essentials necessary for successful selling, it's—all together now—*communication skills*. Yes! (laughter) That's right. You make the sale when the buyer believes, really believes, it is in their best interest to exchange their money for your product. To create this belief, you must have the skills and—that's product or *service*, of course— they must have the philosophy of effective communications. This means that you, the salesperson, must be out there. Touching the minds and the hearts, the hopes and the dreams, the cares and ... In order to accomplish this task you must be aware of several points.

That's how people talk, and this particular presentation was forceful and very well received, with lots of interaction between the speaker and the audience. But on paper the words look flat, clumsy, and—because of the shifts and digressions normal to spontaneous speech—full of grammatical errors. Extract the essence and turn it into strong written language.

> **A literary version:** How do you sell? You *communicate!* You convince potential buyers that whatever you're selling is worth far more than anything else they could ever exchange their money for. To do this, you learn how to talk to their hearts as well as their heads. Here are the five rules for communicating with your customer.

Speakers use: inflections, pauses, shifts in volume, movement, demeanor, facial expression, gestures, eye contact, pacing, and tone of voice.

Writers use: italics, dashes, parentheses, commas, colons, semicolons, ellipses, vergules, capitalization, length of sentences and paragraphs, type sizes, and sometimes even type colors like red headlines.

By using a sarcastic tone of voice, a speaker can indicate a meaning opposite to the words being used. However, sarcasm rarely works on paper. Too often it is taken at face value and interpreted as fact rather than ridicule. If you must dabble in irony, do it carefully and use quotes or capitals: *He, he assured us, was God's Gift to Women* or *He was, he assured us, "God's gift to women."*

Abandon "Hope"

While you are certainly selling hope, the word itself can lead to flabby letter writing. Trainer Ann Bloch, in her lively *Writing Workout!* newsletter, says, "*Hope* is a positive-sounding word—or is it?" She feels it is so overused that it now sounds "weak, unsure, tentative." She offers these examples:

> We hope the enclosed materials will meet your needs. (*But we're not sure.*)

> We hope to meet you in the future. (*Minimally polite, not enthusiastic.*)

> We hope you will call us with any questions you may have. (*Limp.*)

The first word in each of these sentences focuses on the writer, not the reader, because *hope* is a "we-focused" word. Focus instead on the reader:

> You'll find the solution marked on the enclosed fact sheet. (*Positive, with personalized marks on enclosure, focus on "you," the reader.*)

> Let's finally meet each other this summer. (*Focuses on both reader and writer; states specific time.*)

> Questions? Call Marie Downs or me. (*Usual fat removed; alternate name given.*)

Turn your emphasis around by abandoning *hope*.

Don't Repeat Yourself

Repetition is essential for speech, but *anathema* for print. In any good sales presentation, speech, or conversation, the key points are repeated: First you tell them what you're going to tell them, then you tell them, then you tell them what you told them. But repetition on the printed page is unnecessary and counterproductive. The eye provides the necessary reinforcement by jumping back and forth in the text to double check key points, make connections, and review information. Don't repeat yourself. The only exception is in a summary which — contrary to everything you may have been taught — should come at the *beginning* of a letter. So summarize: yes, but repeat: no or with great caution.

Use Action Verbs

A "direct verb" transfers action from one thing to another: Man bites dog. An "indirect verb" is more static: The dog is bitten by the man. In sales letters, direct, active verbs make a stronger impact than indirect, inactive ones.

INACTIVE: Applications should be submitted by May 30.

ACTIVE: Submit the enclosed application by May 30.

INACTIVE: All these details should be discussed at your earliest convenience.

ACTIVE: We need to discuss these details. Would Thursday or Friday be better for you?

INACTIVE: It is no secret that the appearance and quality of an organization's grounds has a direct and significant impact on customers, suppliers, investors and (maybe most importantly) employees.

ACTIVE: The first thing everyone sees when they drive up to Allied's regional headquarters is the grounds — the trees, not the building; the lawns, not the lobby; the flower beds, not the offices and labs. Your landscaping is your first chance to make a lasting impression.

INACTIVE: The value of your home can be drastically reduced by termite infestation.

ACTIVE: .   Termites destroy homes. We destroy termites and save your equity.

In letters and in life, some people feel that indirect statements are more polite. They say, "The garbage needs to be taken out," rather than "Honey, would you take out the garbage?" Or they say, "Switching to our system could have several immediate benefits," rather than "You could benefit immediately if you decide to switch to our system." In some cultures and situations, it is rude to say anything directly, but, in general, straight talk is clearer, more forceful, and ultimately more polite because there is no doubt about what the reader is being asked to decide or do.

Keep It Short and Simple

Use short sentences, short paragraphs, short letters. Be brief. The briefer you are, the more you are in command of the situation and the more likely you are to be read.

Wordy three- and four-page sales letters are a current fad, but who actually reads them? Do your reader and your budget a favor. Stick to one page. If you can't say everything on one page, use enclosures for additional information such as schedules or lists.

On the next page is a *real* letter from an entrepreneur who is offering an interesting new product in a lengthy sales letter. (We've disguised the product.) The BEFORE version was two pages, the text running almost margin to margin in tiny type. The AFTER version is the same letter, condensed to one page. Which do you prefer? (Note that the writer takes 880 words to sell a product that is supposed to condense information and save the user reading time!)

Keep It Short and Simple - BEFORE

Dear

Imagine. You're driving in your car. You slide a cassette into the stereo and in a matter of minutes you hear about the most important events and regulation changes affecting the import/export business this month.

I'm talking about a lively import/export newsletter on tape. Produced by trade experts for trade experts. With the sound of a half-hour radio news program. And rushed to you by overnight delivery twice a month.

It's called the ABROAD-CAST.

And by acting right now you can evaluate four programs RISK-FREE. Plus you'll automatically qualify to receive a $99 Charter Discount off your first year's subscription. I'll share the details with you in just a few minutes, but first...

**Hear how ABROAD-CAST can help
you conquer your reading and gain you time.**

As an exporter, you and I share a problem. Every day, mountains of paper flow into our offices. But the material we get to keep ourselves up-to-date and on our toes — changing regulations, changing carriers and routes, changing costs and duties — usually gets buried within ever-growing reading stacks. (I keep mine on the window sill.)

Frankly, we miss out on a lot of the information that would make us better business people and make our jobs a lot less hectic and more satisfying.

That's why I developed ABROAD-CAST.

**ABROAD-CAST is your most efficient, effective, and enjoyable way
to keep up-to-date on international developments.**

Twenty-two times a year you receive a half-hour newscast with the sound of radio news, produced for ABROAD-CAST on cassette tape.

Here are just a few of the features you hear during very ABROAD-CAST:

- Your program kicks off with a **five-minute headline broadcast**, quickly alerting you to important developments.

- **Focus reports on agencies and specialties** provide you with in-depth analyses of new rules, trends, and other regulatory developments. For exporters, the most recent decisions of regulatory agencies; changes in duties, taxation, trade sanctions, and embargoes; international political and carrier developments; and other such specialties are critical news. ABROAD-CAST gives these topics careful treatment.

- **ABROAD-CAST Digest** brings you concise briefings on the leading export-related stories in print, in trade and lay publications.

- You also hear about your colleagues, your competitors, and maybe even yourself in our profiles of major exporters.

Best of all, <u>you'll actually listen</u> to ABROAD-CAST and <u>you'll like it</u> because...

BEFORE - continued

Page 2

Every half-hour ABROAD-CAST is live. Entertaining. Full of information.
Like a well-produced radio news program for exporters.

ABROAD-CAST brings you something no other publication in the field can deliver. <u>Sound.</u> And with it, spontaneity. Immediacy. Humor. The voices of experts like you.

The world of import-export — from your perspective — in just a half hour!

First class service. Rushed to you 22 times a year.

You and I are busy specialists who, despite the crush, MUST maintain first class quality in all our work. So, at ABROAD-CAST, we've adopted the same high standards <u>and</u> we've included the extra services that make ABROAD-CAST a critical source for busy people like you...

Every issue of ABROAD-CAST is <u>delivered to you promptly and reliably by overnight carrier.</u>
Every issue of ABROAD-CAST comes with <u>a detailed written outline listing the citation of every case, statute, article, and authority mentioned on tape.</u> You won't have to take notes!

Simply, ABROAD-CAST makes more time for you.

The <u>convenience and portability</u> of ABROAD-CASTs help you find more productive time at your desk...and make more productive use of your time on the move. The <u>quality</u> of ABROAD-CAST means you enjoy keeping up to date on export developments!

Think about it. Wouldn't it be great to feel that you were always on top of your game, always up-to-the-minute on developments that concern you, your colleagues and your clients? And wouldn't it be great to keep up-to-date so easily and so enjoyably? Here's how.

Examine four issues of ABROAD-CAST RISK-FREE and SAVE $99

The proof is in the listening. so why not return your Charter Savings Certificate today and decide for yourself? I'll send you four issues of ABROAD-CAST to preview risk-free.

Give them a listen. Discuss them with your colleagues. Then, after you've had a chance to evaluate all four issues, honor the invoice and look forward to receiving 22 ABROAD-CASTS throughout the year plus a handsome library binder to store your ABROAD-CASTS and Outlines. Or, if you're less than pleased — for any reason — simply return your invoice marked "cancel" and owe nothing. But please keep the four risk-free examination cassettes with my compliments. You have absolutely nothing to risk. Nothing to lose.

So how do you begin receiving your four risk-free issues of ABROAD-CAST?

Easy.

Complete and return your Charter Savings Certificate within the next 30 days and you'll SAVE $99 off the regular ABROAD-CAST subscription price. Act now and hear what you've been missing.

Cordially,

P.S.   Why wait for the mail? Call us today and look forward to receiving the first of four risk-free
         issues of ABROAD-CAST, the twice monthly export newscast on audio cassette for exporters
         on the move! Call 1-800 A-ABROAD.

Keep It Short and Simple - AFTER

Dear

I'm betting $99 that I can keep you on top of the constant changes that affect everyone in the export business—and that you'll find this new method pain free and even fun. It's called ABROAD-CAST.

Everything you need to know—on tape. Twice a month, you'll be rushed a lively half-hour newscast, created <u>by</u> export experts <u>for</u> export experts. In your car, home, or office, just pop in the tape and learn the latest about:

- Regulation changes
- Carrier changes
- Import duty changes
- Your colleagues and competitors
- Political, sociological, and meteorological events that can affect you and your business

And you'll get:

- A complete up-to-the-minute review of important newspaper and trade publication articles and commentaries
- A printed *Outline* of each tape, plus a handsome library binder to hold outlines and tapes

Try ABROAD-CAST <u>free</u>. I'll send you the next four programs and an invoice for $99. If you don't find that ABROAD-CAST is worth many times that amount to you—that it doesn't increase your productivity conveniently and pleasurably—then write "cancel" on the invoice and pay nothing. But if you're as pleased as I think you'll be, your $99 payment counts <u>double</u> toward your first year's subscription price.

So why not return the enclosed Charter Savings Certificate card or call 1-800 A-ABROAD within 30 days to take advantage of this no-risk offer?

Cordially,

Which of those two letters would you rather receive, the BEFORE or the AFTER? Which would you find more persuasive? And how many readers do you think actually made it through the original BEFORE version?

Remember that a great sales letter should be like fast food. Be sure your reader can get through it quickly and pleasurably.

Summarize Longer Letters

If you absolutely *must* write a sales letter longer than a page and a half, summarize the contents in the first paragraph if it's appropriate:

> Three Itineraries: We have prepared three different itineraries for you to choose from:
>
> - via San Francisco, Honolulu, Fiji, Melbourne, Perth, Bangkok, New Delhi, Cairo, Paris, New York
>
> - via Anchorage, Tokyo, Seoul, Omsk, Moscow, Oslo, Reykjavik, New York
>
> - via San Juan, Rio de Janiero, Capetown, Calcutta, Singapore, Christ Church, Santiago, Lima, Bogota, New York
>
> Here are the details ...

•   •   •

> Owning your own ALLIED franchise is a big decision, one that you should make only when you know all the facts about your obligations and potential benefits. Every Allied franchisee is responsible for:
>
> 1. Land and property maintenance
> 2. Employee training and management
> 3. Quality control
> 4. Customer relations
> 5. Scheduled franchise payments, plus percentages
>
> **1. Land and Property Maintenance:** Property must be zoned for...

Help your readers to grasp immediately what will be covered in the letter, and why it is important for them to read past page one.

Use Visual Appeal

When you talk, you've got pacing, tone of voice, pauses, eye contact, and body language to communicate. Writing provides similar opportunities: spacing, punctuation, paragraphs, long and short sentences, and highlighted information. Pull the reader along with headings, bulleted lists, and appropriately highlighted information.

Lists are probably the most abused way to present highlighted information in letters. They're an easy way to catch the reader's attention, but too often they really aren't a list at all. *Don't* number things unless they represent:

- A sequence - Do this first, then this, then that.

- A checklist - Bring these five things to the contract signing; I need to know the following three things.

- Different parts of a whole - Your car needs five kinds of service; Here are the four most important features.

Bullets are a powerful way to grab the eye, but you can't cheat with them either. Bulleted items should form an actual list of similar items presented in a similar format, those "parallel structures" that your English teachers nagged you about. Make all bulleted items parts of the same conceptual whole, all subcategories of the same thing. And use the same grammatical structure for each item—all complete sentences, all active or passive verbs, all nouns, or all gerunds.

WRONG:

> We've been a leader in the industry for more than fifteen years. Our success record is unsurpassed.
>
> - First prize in the 1994 International Business Services competition.

WRONG - continued

> • We've been rated Number One by our trade association for the past three years.
>
> • Let us know your needs. We're happy to give you a free estimate.
>
> • My business card is attached.

> More than one third of the businesses in your industry uses our services. Why not you?

Bullet one is a sentence fragment supporting the statement "Our success record is unsurpassed." Sentence fragments (usually lacking a verb) are okay, as long as you are consistent. But, although it also supports the statement, bullet two is a complete sentence with both a subject and a verb. Bullets three and four are also complete sentences, but aren't supports.

RIGHT:

> We've been a leader in the industry for more than fifteen years. Our success record is unsurpassed:
>
> • We won first prize in the 1994 International Business Services competition.
>
> • We've been rated Number One by our trade association for the past three years.
>
> • Our services are used by more than one third of the businesses in your industry.
>
> We'd like to show you what we can do for you. Just let us know your needs. We'll be happy to give you a free estimate.

All these bullets support the statement "Our success record is unsurpassed" and are complete sentences. (NOTE: Enclosed business cards probably don't need to be mentioned, even if you add a list of enclosures at the end.)

Headings: Yes, it's okay to use headings in letters. Just be sure they really are headlines, announcing the news. The test is whether the reader can use them to scan the letter, to preview the contents or to locate key information. Writing headings can have another advantage: often the writer sees ways to organize information more effectively.

BEFORE Headings

Dear

Pet-Hotel is pleased to announce a half-million dollars worth of new features to protect and pamper your pets. We've added a Dog Heaven mini golf course with trained ball tossers in attendance eighteen hours a day. Our grooming salon has ten gently heated drying rooms to avoid chilling and the noise of hand-held dryers that can frighten the sensitive dog.

The Chien-Bowl exercise arena features a heated Olympic-size swimming pool, divided into racing lanes. Swimming lessons are available for younger dogs, and the warm water is excellent for the arthritic joints of older dogs.

Your reptile friends can now be served in our new Jurassic Jungle wing. We can provide an appropriate customized diet for the most exotic and exacting pet. All live food is raised on our own organic farm, guaranteeing it is free of pesticides.

The Stork Club is another new addition, providing full facilities for expectant moms of all species.

Every cat guest will enjoy the Puss-In-Boots Parlor, offering two hours of supervised play daily, conducted by trained animal psychologists. You will be provided with a full analysis of your pet's psychological health when you pick up your animal friend.

We look forward to welcoming your beloved to Pet-Hotel's fabulous new facilities. See you soon.

Cordially,

AFTER Headings

Dear

Pet-Hotel is pleased to announce a half-million dollars worth of new features to protect and pamper your pets.

What's New for Dogs: We've added a Dog Heaven mini golf course with trained ball tossers in attendance eighteen hours a day. Our grooming salon has ten gently heated drying rooms, to avoid chilling and the noisy hand-held dryers that can frighten the sensitive dog. The Chien-Bowl exercise arena features a heated Olympic-size swimming pool, divided into racing lanes. Swimming lessons are available for younger dogs, and the warm water is excellent for the arthritic joints of older dogs.

What's New for Cats: Every cat guest will enjoy the Puss-In-Boots Parlor, offering two hours of supervised play daily, conducted by trained animal psychologists. You will be provided with a full analysis of your pet's psychological health when you pick up your animal friend.

And Now We Love Reptiles Too: Your reptile friends can be served in our new Jurassic Jungle wing. We can provide an appropriate customized diet for the most exotic and exacting pet. All live food is raised on our own organic farm, guaranteeing it is free of pesticides.

Pregnant pets? The Stork Club is another new addition, providing full facilities for expectant moms of all species.

We look forward to welcoming your beloved pet to Pet-Hotel's fabulous new facilities. See you soon.

Cordially,

Highlighting important information in sales letters has traditionally been done with underlining and ALL CAPS. Computers have added **bold face**. Now laser printers offer a candy store of type fonts and sizes, italics, sub-

and super-scripts, even multiple ink colors. The only warning: don't overdo it. When you emphasize everything, you emphasize nothing.

Here are two similar, *real* letters from credit card companies, their identities disguised. (Both were sent on smaller-than-usual paper.) Which one do you find more readable and appealing?

Do you prefer REAL LETTER A's highlighting?

```
            You have been pre-approved
      for the credit card that lets you earn
      both free gasoline and No Annual Fee.
```

```
Dear

Some cards give rewards.  Some cards have no
annual fee.  Some cards save you money and
eliminate the need for other cards.  Now, get
the one card that lets you have it all: The
Allied Kredit Kard from Allied Bank with a
$6,000 credit line.

You benefit even more by receiving Charter
Membership if you respond to this offer by May
1, 1998.  As an Allied Kredit Kard Charter
Member, your new card comes to you with No
Annual Fee for the first year.  In addition, by
using your card for just six purchases each
year, you continue to pay No Annual Fee.

Using it is easy - and automatic.  With the
Allied Kredit Kard, the average driver can save
10% on an annual gasoline bill!  Each year with
your Allied Kredit Kard, you will receive your
first $75 of free Allied gasoline by earning 2%
on almost anything you buy.  You will earn a 1%
bonus on all Allied gasoline purchases.  These
Allied gasoline purchases earn you 3%.  After
you earn your first $75 of free Allied gasoline,
you continue to earn a 1% bonus on Allied
```

gasoline purchases that year. You continue to earn and get free Allied gas year after year!

You can save even more with a **competitive 26.5% Variable Annual Percentage Rate** that gives you affordable buying power around town, or around the world - at restaurants, movies, grocery stores and on vacation. The Allied Kredit Kard is accepted at Allied stations, where you will find the world's best-selling gasoline.

Enjoy many other advantages from the Allied Kredit Kard:
- Acceptance at over 10 million locations
- Access to over 128,000 automated teller machines (ATMs)
- 24-hour customer service
- 25-day grace period for purchases

                                        (over, please)

---------------------- [page two] --------------------------

Respond today! Get the Allied Kredit Kard from Allied Bank, the one card that does what your store cards, gas cards and other cards do, and more — it lets you earn free Allied gasoline.

Sincerely,

Vice President
Allied Bank

P.S. The sooner you complete the enclosed certificate, the sooner you will be earning free Allied gasoline with the only card you will ever need! Sign up today!

Or do you prefer REAL LETTER B's highlighting?

Dear

Take a look at the interest rates on your monthly credit card statements. Then compare the 16%, 17% or even 18% you may be paying now to Allied Kredit Kard's low rate for purchases:

$$9.4\% \text{ Variable APR}$$

THIS IS ONE OF THE LOWEST RATES CURRENTLY OFFERED BY ANY MAJOR CREDIT CARD ISSUER. In fact, it's only 3.4% above the Prime Rate -- which is all you'll pay for one full year. After the first year, you'll still enjoy a very competitive APR -- just 14.4% based on today's rates.

PLUS A HIGH CREDIT LINE. As an Allied Kredit Kard cardmember, you'll enjoy an initial credit line of up to $10,000. How's that for buying power?

AND NO ANNUAL FEE. Unlike many other gold cards, which charge an annual fee as high as $40, this low-APR Allied Kredit Kard has no annual fee.

That's our offer, pure and simple.

(over, please)

----------------------- [page two] -----------------------

But actually, our offer doesn't end there. Because this Allied Kredit Kard comes complete with a number of special benefits you're sure to appreciate.

For example, your new low APR can help you <u>save</u> <u>money on balances you already have with other</u> <u>credit cards</u>. As soon as you become an Allied Kredit Kard member, we'll send you Balance Transfer checks that you can use to transfer higher-rate balances to your new 9.4% variable APR Allied Kredit Kard account.

And as an added convenience, you can actually choose when your Allied Kredit Kard payment is due each month -- so that our schedule fits with yours. Plus, you'll always be able to call our 24-hour Customer Service Center for assistance whenever the need arises.

So take advantage of this unique opportunity and return the enclosed Membership Certificate promptly. The sooner you do, the sooner you could have a low-cost, full-featured Allied Gold Kard from Allied, the bank that's in the business of helping customers manage their finances better.

Sincerely,

P.S. To apply for an Allied Gold Kard with <u>NO</u> <u>ANNUAL FEE</u> and a low, variable APR for purchases that's now just <u>9.4%</u>, complete and return the enclosed certificate today-- this special, limited-time offer expires soon.

You can analyze the effectiveness of these two letters by scanning the highlighted information. How quickly can you grasp the message? Do the highlighted portions tell the story? Can they almost stand alone as an outline or spine of the message?

Highlighted Portions of LETTER A

You have been pre-approved
for the credit card that lets you earn
both free gasoline and No Annual Fee.

The Allied Kredit Kard from Allied Bank with a $6,000
credit line.

No Annual

No Annual Fee.

Using it is easy - and automatic.

These Allied gasoline purchases earn you 3%.

competitive 26.5% Variable Annual Percentage Rate

Enjoy many other advantages from the Allied Kredit
Kard:

Respond today!

Highlighted Portions of LETTER B

9.4% Variable APR

THIS IS ONE OF THE LOWEST RATES CURRENTLY
OFFERED BY ANY MAJOR CREDIT CARD ISSUER.

PLUS A HIGH CREDIT LINE.

AND NO ANNUAL FEE.

save money on balances you already have with
other credit cards.

If you're like most people, you find it easier to scan and understand the
highlights of LETTER B. LETTER A is a jungle of mixed emphasis.

Pacing can be done in print, just as in speech. You can speed up readers with short words, short sentences, short paragraphs. You can slow them down with longer words, sentences and paragraphs. You can pause with dashes — (and ellipses.) You can "raise your voice" by using *italics* or all CAPITAL LETTERS.

WARNING: Avoid writing more than a few words in all-caps! They're much harder to read than upper/lower case and you'll exhaust your reader.

AVOID ALL-CAPS - VERY DIFFICULT TO READ
IT'S VERY TEMPTING TO TRY TO CALL ATTENTION
TO IMPORTANT INFORMATION BY PUTTING IT IN
ALL-CAPITALS, BUT IT JUST CREATES A
HARD-TO-READ, HARD-TO-SCAN BLOCK OF TYPE.
MOST READERS GET TIRED AND GIVE UP.

Stick to upper/lower case - much easier to read
The eye has a much easier time flowing over upper/lower case text. Keep all-caps to a minimum—just a few words at most—and find other ways to show your readers that this block of information is important—

```
Like putting a box around it.
```

Proofread Your Letters:

The fastest way to kill a sale is to address your reader incorrectly. Automatic mailing programs that insert names in key spots can create some goofs that would be funny if they didn't cost you customers. Sheila Murray Bethel has gotten used to occasional letters that call her "Ms. Murraybethel" of "Ms. Bethel," but she balked at one addressing her as "Ms. Sheila Murray Bethel, Chair" that began: "Dear Ms. Chair:" She received another that still had the computerized codes in place, so she was cozily advised that "This is the perfect time, **INSERT *ATIT* ASUR**, to take advantage ..." Don't trust technology. Check your letters before they go out.

The second worst thing you can do is to send out a letter with careless grammatical and spelling errors. A lot of us have come to depend on the spell-checking features of our word processing software, but even that valuable aid has its limits. John Jay Daly of Daly Communications in Chevy Chase, Maryland sent us this humorous reminder:

> Be cuss homonyms in English are sew common, yew mussed be shore to reed vary care full, like in this veers:
>
> I have a spelling checker.
> It came with my PC.
> It plainly Marx for my revue
> Miss steaks I cannot sea.
> I've run this poem threw it.
> I'm sure your please to no,
> Its litter perfect inn it's weigh,
> My checker tolled me sew.

Proofread, proofread, proofread!

Use postscripts—maybe: Remember the TV detective Columbo—"Oh, there's just one more thing." A P.S *can* be the most powerful part of a letter. It used to be that nearly everyone read a short P.S. even if they only scanned the letter. Unfortunately, postscripts have been so overused and abused that they have lost their impact. If you decide to use a postscript:

- Use it wisely!
- Make it a hook to get the reader to go back over the letter.
- *Don't* just repeat something from the body of the letter.

> P.S. Would Thursday or Monday be better?
>
> P.S. The $100 has no strings attached.
>
> P.S. Bob Becknell says "hi," and that he looks forward to seeing you there.

Use enclosures — wisely: You can keep your letters spare, lean, and to the point if you relegate cumbersome schedules, samples, lists of prices, references, etc. to an enclosure. But use common sense.

DON'T add extra pages unnecessarily. Include the information in the body of the letter if that's easier.

DO use prepaid reply envelopes or postcards if appropriate. An especially effective way to get back information you want is to enclose a self-addressed (typed, not pre-printed) envelope with a real, brightly colored postage stamp on it. Fold your letter up so the stamp shows clearly when the letter is opened. Your reader doesn't get a chance to put your letter aside "for later" to find an envelope or stamp. You've made it easier for them to reply than not to. For some reason, most people can't *stand* throwing away an unused stamp. A few will soak the stamps off and reuse them, but most will do what you asked—check off the boxes on a survey or scribble a reply on a card—and stuff it back in your stamped envelope, just to get it off their desks. It's relatively expensive, but it works! (TIP: #9 envelopes enclose neatly inside a #10 business envelope without folding, yet will hold standard letter-size paper.)

DO be sure that information the reader may need in the future—your address, phone number, key dates, etc.—is on the part of your mailing that the reader keeps, *not* on the back of a tear-off coupon or only on a send-away postcard.

DON'T enclose unrelated "cute" items:

- "Chew on these facts" - stick of gum
- "No more headaches" - aspirin
- "No sweeter deal" - candy

This approach is dated, trivializes your product, is condescending to the intelligence of the reader, and may backfire if the item arrives damaged or destructs all over the reader's lap, desk, or carpet. You may even be presented with a cleaning bill.

Use Humor Warily

Everyone claims they love a sense of humor—but there's nothing more individual and less universal than what makes people laugh. One person's joke is another's outrage. In 1994, the Lawyers Travel Service ran an ad in the *Wall Street Journal* with a photo of Abraham Lincoln and a headline, "Never underestimate the consequences of a bad seat assignment." The travel agency's Marketing Director ruefully told *Advertising Age* that they had been bombarded with "emotional and somewhat negative" calls and letters from "incensed" readers who swore they would never become clients.

This ill-advised attempt at humor cost a company business. Here's another example that might easily have cost a life. Marianna Nunes, a popular speaker on "Humor in the Workplace," was handed the following letter by an eager but misguided salesperson:

Humor gone terribly wrong: The original fills a sheet of paper with giant print, as if hand lettered.

```
Don't be alarmed, this is
a sales call.

Do exactly as I say & nobody gets hurt.

I am armed with a briefcase full of
highly flammable brochures and pencils
containing highly toxic lead.

I also have business cards and
I'm not afraid to use them if I have to.

Please get your Human Resources
Manager or there will be trouble.
```

Anyone who has read a newspaper lately will realize what might happen if someone walked into an office and handed that note to an employee. It could result in a lot of things—hastily summoned security guards with drawn guns, a heart attack, an arrest, even flying bullets—but probably not a sale.

What the terrified recipient of this fake hold-up note might see is:

```
Don't be alarmed, this is
a sales call.

Do exactly as I say & nobody gets hurt.

I am armed with a briefcase full of
highly flammable brochures and pencils
containing highly toxic lead.
```

I also have business cards and
I'm not afraid to use them if I have to.

Please get your Human Resources
Manager or **there will be trouble.**

This poorly conceived "sales letter" is similar to shouting "Fire!" in a crowded theater and could get a similar reaction.

Humor that irritates: Failed attempts at humor may be dangerous, but more often they are just unproductive. For example, would you be moved to buy from the author of this real but disguised letter? Do you find it droll? Or irritating?

```
Dear

How's By Youse?

Tis us...da Fokes from Fan-Tastik Koolers wit annudder
triffic idea for Keepin Yu Kool.  Our nu 18" Power-Fan
mounts in and winder and is poifect for the hot daze
ahed.  Or what about a mini 3" pursnall fan that hangs
rite around yur nek?

So listen...who ain't been out to visit our
Fan-Tastick Kooler showroom yet?  Ain't gonna
tell...huh?  OK...so you're invited.  Come visit.
We'll talk.  Yule see over 200 sooper fans for all yur
koolin needs.  Who loves ya?  We do!

See ya!
```

(Contributed -- but **NOT** written -- by Jeff Powell of Edward Don & Company)

Using What You Have Learned - BEFORE and AFTER Examples

On the following pages are three typical sales letters in BEFORE and AFTER versions. Each BEFORE is a *real* letter, disguised to hide the product or service of the sender, but otherwise word for word and paragraph for paragraph like the original. Scan each of these BEFOREs and decide how you would improve it. Then see what we did in an AFTER rewrite.

BEFORE - Original

Dear

The USPS reports a dramatic increase in the use of Certified Mail by many offices like yours. It's the most effective way to obtain the necessary hard copy ***"proof of receipt"*** on critical documents and date sensitive notifications. Unfortunately, the downside of mailing legal correspondence via *"First Class - Certified Mail, Return Receipt Requested"* is the inordinate amount of time you must spend completing the Postal Service's burdensome certified mail paperwork.

We have a better way! We are proud to be the exclusive provider of the Supra Certified Mailer. This cleverly designed form saves over **75%** of the time and effort required to prepare a piece of certified correspondence. This form is fully approved for use in the US Mail and simplifies the entire preparation process. Our form can be used in a "low tech" typewriter or easily automated using your existing software.

In addition, our form incorporates a **charge back slip** that makes Cost Recovery a part of each and every certified mail preparation! This allows your law firm to process more matters more efficiently and this positively affects the firm's gross income. This is sure to please management in small, midsize, and large businesses as well.

If your office sends more than 3 notifications at a time via Certified mail, or you know of one that does, you owe it to yourself to try a "no obligation" **evaluation kit**. Just send back the enclosed card, or call our "Certified Mail Hotline" at 1-800-000-0000, and allow me to show you a way to save time and become more cost effective in the preparation of your certified mail.

Sincerely,

Joe Jones
Certified Mail Specialist

P.S. Come see our exhibit at the Annual Association Convention, City Center Hall, on September 3-5.

AFTER - Rewrite

Dear

If your department routinely sends items by "First Class - Certified Mail, Return Receipt Requested," here's what we can save you:

- <u>75% of the time</u> you are now spending.

- <u>Cold, hard cash</u> — We'll figure out exactly how much when you return the enclosed card or call our toll free number, 1-800 000-0000. There's no obligation.

<u>How we make USPS faster and cheaper</u>. Of course USPS Certified Mail continues to be your most effective tool for getting hard-copy Proofs of Receipt on critical documents and date-sensitive notifications, but it has a definite downside: the time it takes you to complete the USPS's burdensome paperwork.

Now we have a better way! We are proud to be the exclusive provider of the simplified Supra Certified Mailer, fully approved for use in the U.S. Mail. It even has a Charge Back Slip that makes cost recovery routine. Our form can be used in a "low-tech" typewriter or easily automated, using your existing software.

Sincerely

Joe Jones
Certified Mail Specialist

P.S. Come see our exhibit at the Annual Association Convention, City Center Hall, on September 3-5.

NOTE: The BEFORE starts with a once-upon-a-time history of the problem. The AFTER's purpose is in the first sentence. The BEFORE stresses features ("exclusive provider of the Supra Certified Mailer" - "cleverly designed" - "approved for use in the US Mail"). The AFTER letter is shorter and stresses the benefits (save time and money).

BEFORE - Original

RE: SIMPLIFIED STRATEGIC PLANNING

Dear

The foremost responsibility of Executive Management is to define the mission and chart the overall course and direction for the company. There is no substitute for a well-defined strategy that can help your organization do the right things, in the right place, at the right time.

The Center for Simplified Strategic Planning has pioneered a streamlined methodology which is highly workable for the small to mid-sized company. It has been under progressive development since 1981 and has been successfully applied in hundreds of companies. State University has been proud to present this highly acclaimed program since 1982. It has consistently received high evaluations from over 4,000 attendees.

Whether you are new to strategic planning or experienced, attending this extraordinary seminar can be one of the most important things you do this year. We strongly urge you to review the enclosed program announcement bulletin and to contact the seminar coordinator at (800) 000-0000 , to register TODAY.

We look forward to having you as a participant in one of our presentations of this unique seminar.

Sincerely,

John Waverly

Enclosure

AFTER - Rewrite

Dear

If you can do just <u>one</u> important thing for yourself and your company this year, it probably should be our highly acclaimed

SIMPLIFIED STRATEGIC PLANNING Seminar
for small to mid-sized companies

Why strategic planning? You <u>have</u> to do it, but how? On top of everything else you have to do every day, you're responsible for defining the mission and charting the course and direction of your company — for doing everything right, in the right place, at the right time.

We make it easy: The Center for Simplified Strategic Planning has pioneered a streamlined formula especially for the small to mid-sized company. Whether you're an experienced planner or not, you'll come out with powerful new perspectives and tools.

Why it works: Since 1981, our system has been applied successfully by hundreds of companies. State University has been proud to present our program since 1982. More than 4,000 attendees have given us high evaluations.

Convenient schedule: You can choose from day, evening, or weekend seminars. Pick the best time in the enclosed program bulletin. Then call the seminar coordinator ASAP at (800) 000-0000 to ensure your place.

Sincerely,

John Waverly

Enclosure

NOTE: Despite BEFORE's heading, "SIMPLIFIED STRATEGIC PLANNING," it's not until paragraph three of the original that the reader learns the purpose of the letter: to announce a seminar. Headings in the AFTER version also improve readability, highlighting information and pulling the reader along.

BEFORE - Original

Dear Account Holder:

On behalf of everyone at First Priam Bank, I would like you to know that we are excited to be a new part of your community. Even though you may have heard that Ulysses Bank is becoming part of First Priam Bank, you probably still have questions about who we are, the financial services we will offer, and how we will meet your banking needs. The enclosed information will help answer many of those questions.

The story of First Priam Bank is simple. It's about people and progress, about 75 years of strength and service. It's about people who have a genuine commitment to serving customers with personal attention and financial knowledge. We hope you see that commitment in every encounter you have with First Priam.

A few special points of interest to you:

● Enclosed are two booklets. One provides you with important information that will show you how Ulysses services will become First Priam Bank services. The other contains legal information regarding your accounts and a schedule of fees. First Priam's fees are not only lower in most cases, but also there are many options to avoid paying fees.

● Within the week you'll receive a comprehensive catalog detailing all of First Priam's financial services. Please retain the enclosed booklets and the catalog for future reference.

● On December 10th, you may begin banking at any First Priam office and enjoy the convenience of more than 1,300 offices from Baltimore to Key West. First Priam signs will also begin to appear on Ulysses Bank branches in your neighborhood and throughout the state.

We know that the coming weeks will be a time of transition for you and for all of us. We also understand that you may have questions. Please feel free to call on us any time at any location, or to telephone our toll-free information line at 1-800-000-0000. It will be our pleasure to hear from you. We thank you for the opportunity to serve you, and we look forward to the chance to earn your business every single day.

Sincerely,

AFTER - Rewrite

Dear Account Holder:

As you may have heard, Ulysses Bank is becoming part of First Priam Bank. Two enclosed booklets provide important information about some of the changes, and within the week you'll receive a comprehensive catalogue of all First Priam's financial services. In the meantime, you probably want to know exactly what these changes will mean to <u>you</u>.

<u>What will be the same</u>:

- All your Ulysses accounts and services are unaffected.

- You can continue to use all your Ulysses checkbooks, passbooks, loan payment coupons, etc. (Replacements with the First Priam Bank insignia will be issued when you need new ones.)

- You can continue to bank at your familiar Ulysses Bank branches. (First Priam signs will begin to appear on Ulysses branches in your neighborhood and throughout the state.)

<u>What will be different</u>:

- Starting December 10, you can also use any of First Priam's 1,300 branches, from Baltimore to Key West.

- Many fees will now be lower. (Check the enclosed schedule.)

- You'll also find many more options to avoid paying fees.

We know that you may have questions during the coming weeks. Please feel free to call on us any time at any location, or call our toll-free information line at 1-800 000-0000. We'll be pleased to hear from you.

Sincerely,

P.S. Please keep these two booklets, plus the catalogue you'll get next week, for future reference.

Note: You get home from work after an exhausting day and find this letter from your bank in your pile of mail. How much time and energy are you willing to devote to figuring out what they want you to do? Do you want to read about what nice people they think they are? Probably you just want to know: What's going to be the same? What's going to be different? Our AFTER highlights the answers to these questions. It also uses a P.S. to highlight the bank's request to hang on to the informational literature.

Consider a Postcard

Even the busiest prospect will take a moment to read a postcard. Popular speaker Alan Cimberg is a postcard fan: "Its weakness — you can't get too much on it — is also its strength — it's a quick read. You can drop a letter unopened in the wastebasket but nearly everyone scans a postcard."

FROM THE DESK OF:

BILL BETHEL

Walt, WHAT A GReat LuNCh !!! How CAN I THANK you? Congrodulations on your Company Growth Last quarter. I AM glad to have been a part of it. Now, How can I help more? phone and we can plan it.

1376 Vancouver Avenue ▪ Burlingame, CA 94010 ▪ (415) 344-1747

(actual size: 8.5" x 3.5")

A postcard can be especially effective for those important quick responses and thank-you's that build so much goodwill. They save secretarial time and provide a personal touch. If you need a record of what was said, photocopy each communication for your clients' files or note the contents in their word processor file.

You might want to have special cards printed up. (Check with the U.S. Postal Service for any current size restrictions.)

The Empty Envelope

Top insurance salesman Tom Dashiell says that when he's tried and tried to get an appointment and all else fails, he sends an empty envelope, best quality stationery, of course, with his name prominent in the return address. "Invariably they call to find out what was supposed to be inside," he says, "but you can only do this once."

When Is It Better *NOT* to Write?

Don't send anything you've written when you're really mad. (Angry or sarcastic words are like pizza. They taste awful the next day.) Don't send anything you've written when you're depressed or really tired. Some of your negativity is bound to creep into your approach and attitude. And don't write when you're not going to have time to follow up. Each letter is like a seed that needs tending. Even if you don't plan to pursue the recipients by telephone or personal visit, at the very least keep careful records of responses. What worked? What didn't?

The Importance of Follow-Through

Bill Bethel has a popular new training program called *Communicating with Your Customer.* He sent 108 cold query letters describing this program to the sales manager members of the Sales and Marketing Executives Association. No one returned the enclosed reply card. Then Bill phoned fifteen names from the list. Eventually he got through to five of them. Not one remembered receiving his letter. Let's look at the letter that failed and how this changed Bill's follow up.

The Letter That Didn't Work

Dear

Did any of your salespeople ever walk away from a sales interview shaking his or her head saying, "He just didn't get it"? Or, "I couldn't make her understand"?

When a sale isn't made, often it's not because the product wasn't needed, wanted or affordable, but because the salesperson just didn't connect with the potential buyer.

After all, isn't selling the art of making a connection with a prospect that influences a favorable decision? That's what my program is all about: teaching your salespeople and other customer-contact people how to connect with your customers.

No one is born knowing the right moment to ask the right question, to make the perfect statement, or to listen intently to the customer. We have to <u>learn</u>. Everyone can learn to communicate, to persuade, influence, and negotiate to a successful sale. Won't you let me tell you how my program can make a major difference in the gross volume and net profit of your sales force?

Sincerely,

Bill Bethel

P.S. Please phone, FAX, or mail me the attached card to let me know the best time to meet.

What went wrong? Bill had composed the letter more or less "on automatic," using all the techniques that had worked so well over the years. Obviously something had changed. He sat down to analyze. The tight economy had meant that most companies have cut back on or eliminated training programs and the "frills" of having high-profile speakers at company events, but the top trainers continued to have full schedules. Had the letter gone to the wrong people? Bill decided not. At the wrong time of year? (Expenses that must be budgeted a year or more in advance mean certain buying decisions are geared to the calendar.) Again, no. Was price a factor? No, price was not mentioned in the letter or the accompanying brochure.

Bill decided to approach these busy men and women again with a shorter letter, plus enclosures of a brochure and reply card. As a further experiment, he randomly divided the list in half and sent a different letter to each half. Here they are:

Second Attempt #1

Dear

Why should you hire Bill Bethel in the fall of 1994?

1995!

Sincerely,

Bill Bethel

Second Attempt #2

Dear

Can you talk your salespeople into increasing sales? *I* can.

May I prove it to you?

Sincerely,

Bill Bethel

Bill then logged his responses. No one responded directly to letter #1, but 100 percent of the recipients remembered the letter when Bill reached them on the phone, and several made appointments.

Letter #2, which had contained a brochure describing specific speeches, had two immediate requests for more information. One of these respondents booked four speeches within days after the mailing went out. Obviously, part of this is random luck—Bill's letter arrived at just the right time to generate this new client. However, the letter got noticed, not tossed, and the reader's reaction was positive. Ninety-nine percent of "luck" is the hard work and intelligence to put yourself in a position for positive things to happen.

Follow-Through Checklist

When a letter doesn't get the response you want, go back and figure out why:

• Did your letter/s go to the right person? Are you sure that this person has the power to buy? The interest?

• Did you grab the reader in the first sentence or two while making it clear why you were writing?

• Should you try emphasizing a different benefit or motivation? Did you address the most important features and benefits from your potential customer's point of view?

• Did you confront and overcome potential objections?

• Was your letter easy to read?

• Was the tone of your letter appropriate for your product or service and your readers?

• Was your letter too long? Too short?

Keep track of what works and what doesn't. It isn't always possible to know exactly why a particular letter doesn't get a strong response, but if you analyze the success of each communication, a pattern will emerge eventually.

4
Ready to Use Letters

If you send out five selling letters or notes to current and potential customers every business day, five days a week, fifty weeks a year, that's 1,250 contacts every year—1,250 opportunities to connect with your customers. Bill Bethel calls this *The Magic Five* of sales letters. And it's not as hard as you think.

A sales letter can be the classic prospecting letter, but that's not the only way you sell. You sell every time you respond quickly to inquiries and to your prospects' and customers' problems and concerns. You sell when you can turn someone down and give them a boost at the same time. You sell when you recognize people's accomplishments with congratulations, their contributions with thanks, their setbacks and losses with sympathy. Some of this you'll do in person or on the phone, of course, but be sure to put it in writing too. A letter is a tangible reminder of your interest or concern.

THE MAGIC FIVE

Set aside a time each day to write letters. Answer your mail first. Respond immediately to questions and problems. Then take a few minutes to send short individual notes to your customers and potential customers, your colleagues, your suppliers, anyone you do business with. Acknowledge achievements, pass along relevant news, commiserate about difficulties, offer referrals, or just say "Hi."

Once a week, schedule a larger block of time to plan and follow up on your prospecting and cultivating letters. How do you rate the effectiveness and progress of individual contacts, of larger mailings, of your assembling and use of mailing lists? What could be better? Take the time to keep records of responses. Otherwise, you're like a farmer who scatters seeds around but never comes back to see what grew.

This chapter is devoted to sample sales letters for all aspects of selling. A few are real letters, used with the permission of their authors. You can customize these letters to your particular situation, product or service. Or you can use them as inspiration and models for creating your own letters to communicate with your customers clearly and persuasively.

The letters are presented in the following sequence. If you need to locate a particular kind of letter quickly—how to respond to a complaint, say, or a letter to welcome a new customer— you can check the Table of Contents or the Index at the back of the book. Here's a preview:

PROSPECTING LETTERS
    Use checklists
    Paint a vivid picture
    Pose and answer questions
    Stress benefits
        and motivations
    Address a problem
    Overcome objections
    Use a "To Do" list
    Issue an invitation
    Fund raising
    To people attending
        a convention
    Resell a past customer
    The two-step approach
    Use the personal touch
    Stress exclusivity
    Ask for a meeting
    Ask for a phone
        interview
    Ask for interview
        when all else fails
    Ask for a reply
    Ask for letters of
        recommendation
    Ask for referrals

DEVELOPING PROSPECTS
    AND CUSTOMERS
    Answer queries
    Respond to complaints
    Apologizing
    Keeping customers active
    Announcing price increases
    Explaining delays and
        cancellations

SAYING THANKS
    For interview
    For contact at convention
    For referral
    For your business
    Welcome to a new customer
    For a good job
    When it's hard to do

CONGRATULATIONS
    On published article
    On new job
    On promotion
    On retirement

MAKING ANNOUNCEMENTS
    Of a name change
    Of a change of policy
    Of an event
    Or personnel changes
    Of a death

SAYING "NO" NICELY
    Refusing donation
    Refusing invitation
    Refusing credit

COMPLAINING
    To a customer
    To a supplier

CULTIVATING AND
FOLLOW-UPS
    Ticklers and postcards
    Retaining customers
    Recapturing customers
    Contacting cooled-off hot
        prospects

HOW TO USE THIS CHAPTER

Some of the letters you're about to look at are fill-in-the-blanks "generic" letters and some are quite specific to a product or service. A few are real letters, used with the permission of their writers. The generic letters use brackets [like this] to show where you can fill in your own information—for example, [date] or [describe problem]. The specific letters demonstrate approaches to a wide variety of situations.

The letters offer ideas to stimulate your own thinking. You can select a paragraph here and a sentence there, customizing them to fit your needs. Don't limit yourself to letters about your own product or service. You may be selling basketballs and find just the approach you want in a letter about banking or health clubs.

In most of these examples, the writer works for ALLIED, an imaginary and extraordinary conglomerate that operates in just about every area of commerce. ALLIED's letters are addressed to a reader at XYZ, which also has far-flung interests.

Use this chapter as a reference for specific types of letters, or just browse, scanning for ideas and suggestions.

PROSPECTING LETTERS

Keep your prospecting letters to one page, unless you are sure of your reader's interest. Few people will read a letter that takes them more than a minute if they don't know the sender. If you absolutely must offer a lot of information, start by grabbing attention with a very short letter, then put supports, technical information, background, schedules, or prices in an enclosure.

PROSPECTING - Spark reader's thinking with a checklist

Dear

Just one phone call, and we'll solve MOST of your gift-giving problems.

We create ready-to-go and customized gift baskets for your clients, suppliers, coworkers, friends, and family. Choose from our catalogue, or consult with one of our expert stylists to design your own basket.

Our June selections include:

[ ] Congratulations!
[ ] Thanks for your help
[ ] Special World Series baskets
[ ] Father's Day
[ ] Graduation
[ ] Birthday
[ ] Anniversary
[ ] Shower gifts
[ ] New baby
[ ] Retirement
[ ] Get well

Any quantity - Order one basket or 10,000.

Plain or lavish - We'll make your basket as simple or as elaborate as you wish.

Two hour delivery is available for most items. Call us at 1-333 000-0000 and let us help make all your special times even more special.

Sincerely,

PROSPECTING - Spark reader's thinking with a checklist

Dear

What is the primary job of your salespeople?

[ ] To know the stock?
[ ] To present a positive image of the company?
[ ] To handle paperwork efficiently?
[ ] To increase sales?

If you answered "To increase sales," and if I could prove to you that my training technique has already done just this for dozens of companies similar to yours, when would you want to learn more about it?

<u>If</u> you say "now," you can call me at 1-800-548-8001. In just a few minutes we can go over your needs and I'll explain how I can help.

Sincerely,

Bill Bethel

P.S. Don't take my word for it. Look at the enclosed list of recommendations].

PROSPECTING - Paint a vivid picture

Use your creative writing skills to make an unforgettable picture of your reader interacting with your product.

Dear

Visualize this. You're approaching your house on a dark night and suddenly all the lights go on and a scanner tells you if anyone is in your house or yard.

I'm talking about a new device called **SafeHouse** that lets you come home to comfort and safety with just the press of a button. And you can reverse the process when you leave, turning off the lights once you have locked the door, descended the steps, and left the yard. Amazingly, **SafeHouse** weighs just 4 oz. and fits in pocket or purse.

If you send me the enclosed reply card by June 2, you can try **SafeHouse** free for 30 days. You have nothing to risk. Nothing to lose. And maybe a lot to gain.

Sincerely,

PROSPECTING - Paint a vivid picture

Dear

The expedition ship POLE STAR will spend two unforgettable weeks in November voyaging in the waters of Costa Rica and

Panama. Please join us aboard this 100-passenger ship as we explore luxuriant rain forests, tranquil uninhabited islands, dazzling coral gardens, thriving native cultures, and, of course, the legendary Panama Canal.

Costa Rica is one of the most biologically diverse countries in the world and a leader in nature conservation. In its justly famous national parks, you will see iridescent hummingbirds and rare scarlet macaws, three-toed sloths and spider monkeys. You will explore isolated white-sand beaches and navigate dense forest-lined rivers, home to a wide variety of wading birds.

Panama is no less intriguing, offering a look at the cultures of this region. As you venture into the tropical rain forest, you will be greeted by the Choco Indians, who only recently have begun contact with the outside world.

In the San Blas Islands of the Caribbean, we will visit the home of the Kuna Indians, famous for their riotously colorful fabrics.

Panama Canal: A highlight of our voyage will be our two crossings of the Panama Canal, one by day and one during the evening—riveting experiences that you will never forget. At night, the passage is simply magical, with much of the Canal and the adjacent rain forest illuminated.

Exploring under water: Snorkeling equipment is available on board and we carry our own glass-bottomed boat, so the vibrant undersea world is at your feet.

Book now. Call me or Nancy Coogan at 000 000-0000 for reservations or if you have any questions about the trip.

Sincerely,

PROSPECTING - Pose and answer questions

A Basic Format

Dear

Your need for _____ has never been so critical. Now there is a proven, successful way to [do it/avoid it]. It's the XYZ [name of product or service].

[Then ask reader three or four questions, such as ...]

Why is XYZ different?

- Describe
- Describe

Who needs XYZ?

- One sentence case history of company that suffered because they didn't have XYZ.
- One sentence case history of a second company that because they didn't have XYZ.

Who already uses it?

- List
- List

How much money can you save?

[Provide chart, figures]

How can you learn more? Just return the enclosed postcard or call me at 800-000-0000.

Sincerely,

An Example

Dear Ms. Mosetich:

With the recent outbreaks of dangerous Lyme Disease, your need for tick protection for yourself and your family has never has never been so critical. Now there is a proven, successful way to rid your yard and grounds of ticks <u>for three months</u>. It's the **Allied Tick-Kicker** and it's guaranteed!

Why is the Tick-Kicker different?

- No poisons to endanger your children and pets. **Tick-Kicker** attracts ticks with special low-frequency sounds and kills them dead with microwaves.

- No disruption of native ecology. Only ticks are affected.

Who already uses the Tick-Kicker? The City and County of Middleville, the East State Park Authority, and the Association of Day Camps have all mandated the use of Tick-Kicker for the past three years.

What proof do you have? Three independent studies have shown that Tick-Kicker is 100% effective in eliminating ticks for a minimum of three months. (We'll provide full test data on request.)

How can you learn more? Just return the enclosed postcard or call me at 800-000-0000.

Sincerely,

PROSPECTING - Stress benefits

Dear

If your firm has new hires, interns, or business associates coming to the Denver area, we can *save you half the cost* of the average hotel room!

The March 1999 issue of *Business Travel* (copy enclosed) says that the average daily cost of accommodations is $148.23, plus $68.49 for food, an average total cost of $216.72 per person per day.

We offer short-term, fully furnished, spacious apartments throughout the metropolitan area as an affordable, convenient, and home-like alternative for people on the move. Corporate billing is acceptable.

Our apartments provide twice the space and comfort of an average hotel room and feature fully equipped kitchens with cooking and dining utensils, linens (for bath and bed), televisions with cable service, local phone service, and telephone answering machines. Weekly maid service is included at select properties.

In addition, guests can enjoy a range of sports and recreational facilities -- among them swimming pools, spas, tennis courts, and fitness centers -- AT NO EXTRA COST.

While rates vary according to size of apartment, length of stay, and extra services provided, <u>the cost is generally less than half the cost of the average hotel room</u>!

Give us a call today at 1-800-000-0000 or send us a FAX at 000-000-0000 for further information or for reservations.

Sincerely,

ENCL: *Business Travel* article,
        "Your Home in Denver"

NOTE: Always list any enclosures at the end of your letters. It is a guide for whoever is assembling the letter, it provides a future record of what was sent, and it helps to grab attention and steer readers past page one.

PROSPECTING - Stress benefits

Ask yourself:
"How could I better invest $900

Dear

One $900 payment now can save $10,000 or more.

Few people like to think about how much it's going to cost them to die. Some assume that Social Security will pay for everything. But Social Security pays a death benefit of just $255, and only to qualified dependents. That's hardly enough to cover the cost of the simplest funeral.

You can make sure that your survivors aren't left with the difficulties, uncertainties, and expenses of your final arrangements. With CHARON's Exit-Plan, a one-time $900 fee guarantees:

> • Complete peace of mind. Every expense is covered, including transportation, all necessary documents, cremation, and scattering of the ashes.

> • No cost increase <u>ever</u>. Your $900 fee is invested to grow until you have need of our services.

- Unparalleled service. When the time comes, one phone call brings us immediately to home or hospital, any hour, anywhere.

- No difficult and complicated paperwork for your survivors to cope with. We do it all!

- Memorial facilities and grief counseling available.

- You decide now exactly what arrangements you wish. We carry them out when the time comes.

Think about it. You can make your decisions now, or others can make them for you later.

Sincerely,

PROSPECTING - Stress benefits and motivations

Dear

We hate cleaning as much as you do. That's why we started Allied Comprehensive Cleaning Services, an exceptional service for fastidious people. ACCS has a *spotless* three-year record of providing superior housekeeping services to the most discriminating families.

No Hassles!

- Never again will you have to scrub, vacuum, dust, clean, polish, disinfect, deodorize, launder, sort, mend, or wax!

- No complicated record keeping, no payroll deduction or unemployment insurance forms to file. We handle it all.

- No interviewing, hiring, checking references, finding replacements. Just one phone call guarantees that our skilled professionals arrive whenever you want them, on a regular schedule or as needed.

- No fear of loss. All our professionals are fully bonded and insured against damage or loss of any kind.

<u>No Guilt</u>!

• All cleaning products used are nontoxic and absolutely environmentally safe. We use no harmful cleaners or solvents.

• All our employees are well-paid professionals who receive full medical and dental benefits, plus two weeks paid vacation each year. Their high level of satisfaction is reflected in their exceptional service, dedication, and helpful attitude.

Enclosed is a brochure explaining our service in more detail. May we have the pleasure of offering you further information?

Sincerely,

ENCL: "Clean Forever: Your Answer to Dirt and Disorder"

PROSPECTING - Stress benefits and motivations

Dear

> "Reduced Interface Pressure"
> "Product Efficacy"
> "Increased Blood Flow"
> "Reduced Skin Shear"

These are all terms to describe the benefits of using state-of-the-art Mattress Replacement Systems and seating products.

However, the performance of your product is dependent solely upon the composite result of all the components that make up your produce to reduce the incidence or or heal decubitus ulcers. We at Allied-MedTex, Inc. understand the challenges that face a manufacturer in today's market. That's why we have created **Bounce-Back**, the latest technological advance in medical textiles.

Bounce-Back is a textile solution to a serious design challenge: to make a cushioning surface that supports without increasing interface pressures. What is needed is a textile product that conforms to the shape of the supported body part, acting almost as if it is not there at all! However, it must have the ability to return to its original condition -- in other words, **IT MUST BOUNCE BACK**. The ability to stretch without bouncing back creates the potential for "hammocking" and the reduction in product life.

If you are looking for an innovative solution to a problem and are tired of "stopgap" measures, then give us a call at your earliest convenience at 1-800 000-0000.

Sincerely,

PROSPECTING - Address a problem

Dear

Just when you thought you had your payroll system set up to run smoothly through the end of the year, the government has changed the regulations. *PayMaster*, with more than twenty years as the state's leading payroll consultant, is ready to advise medium and small businesses on how to negotiate this new mine field of payroll reporting and deductions.

Why not let our *Paymaster* professionals show you how to comply with the new laws on:

> • Health-coverage reporting, an enormous undertaking that can be reduced to manageability with prudent planning.

> • Voluntary and involuntary deduction requirements, a leading contender for payroll disaster.

> • The accelerated deposit rule which may give your company only one day to figure and deposit payroll taxes.

Perhaps your people have the time and expertise to research and implement these regulatory changes so that you'll avoid expensive losses and penalties. If not, we stand ready serve you.

Sincerely,

PROSPECTING - Address a problem

Start by alerting your reader to problem, then offer highlighted, easy-to-spot alternative actions or solutions. A reader can grasp the gist of the following letter in just a few seconds.

Dear

You may already know that interest rates have increased significantly in the last several weeks. The Chairman of the Federal Reserve has stated that he will seek to keep short-term interest rates "moving up" in order to curb inflation.

If you have not had the opportunity to consider refinancing your home, now is the time to do so.

IF YOU HAVE AN ADJUSTABLE RATE MORTGAGE...

This is an ideal time to reduce your monthly mortgage payment margin substantially by refinancing into a new Adjustable Rate Mortgage.

IF YOU HAVE A FIXED RATE MORTGAGE...

And your present interest rate exceeds 7.5%, you may be able to save quite a bit of money on a monthly basis by choosing a two-step mortgage.

If you would like us to analyze your potential savings without any obligation, please call me at 000-0000.

Sincerely,

PROSPECTING - Address a problem

Dear

Is floor space a problem in your library? Do you need more shelving capacity or more study space?

We can create it for you. Allied Shelf Systems are already used by some of the most prestigious libraries and corporations in the world.

May we show you how Allied Shelf Systems could work for you, at no cost or obligation? Our toll-free number is 1-800 000-0000.

Sincerely,

ENCL: "High Density Mobile Storage"

PROSPECTING - Address a problem

Dear

Where have all your YUPPY customers gone?

They've turned into <u>MUPPIES</u> — Middle-aged Urban Professionals, who now form a rapidly growing 45- to 54-year-old age group. According to the Bureau of Statistics, the number of YUPPIES is due to decline 17% in the next decade, while MUPPIES will <u>increase 50%</u>.

Are you ready to address the changing needs of your customers? Allied Financial Services is sponsoring an industry-wide, two-day seminar on:

The MUPPY Market in the Next Decade:

How to Woo It, Win It, Wow It

Friday-Saturday, May 10-11

Hotel Midlands, East Lessing

In the current volatile economic conditions, some firms are going to fail. A business that understands the challenges will be ready to claim the market share of these weaker companies.

Schedule and registration forms are enclosed. If you need further information, call me at 1-000 000-0000.

Sincerely,

PROSPECTING - Overcome objections

Here's a persuasive, well-organized letter that can get away with requiring more than one page. The headings quickly pull the reader through the various objections and the writer's solutions.

Dear

Your $1,000 rent check can cover a $158,000+ home loan. Today's incredible buyers' market is **your** best chance to buy a home. With interest rates so affordably low, your monthly mortgage will probably be less than you now pay for rent.

Your rent payment of	Covers a loan of *
$600/month	$94,900
$800/month	$126,550
$1,000/month	$158,200
$1,200/month	$189,850

* BASED ON **A.P.R.** OF 6.795%

Don't let lack of information stand between you and your first home. Why wait when you can afford more now?

"I don't have enough for a down payment."

Conventional financing is now available to qualified buyers with as little as 5% down -- and 2% of that amount can be from gifts. FHA loans are available with 3% down payment, and VA loans with nothing down.

"I'm waiting until I can afford something nicer."

With interest rates at record lows, you can probably qualify for that nicer home now. Keep in mind that if interest rates go up just a few percentage points, you will pay hundreds of dollars more each month to borrow the same amount of money. Qualifying for a higher monthly payment will also require a larger income.

"I'm waiting to see if prices go down more."

Home prices have been stable for some time now. As the market continues to recover, you can expect higher prices and less affordable interest rates. By buying now, the cycle of recovery will work in your favor, as the home you own appreciates in value.

"Finding out how much I can afford takes a lot of time and paperwork."

You can be pre-qualified within minutes in any of our offices. A mortgage representative will use a lap-top computer to show you what mortgage amount you qualify for, based on your answers to a few simple questions. As a pre-qualified buyer, you can home-shop with confidence.

Tell us what you now pay for monthly rent. You'll get back a print-out showing how much that payment can buy you today, plus some sample listings in that price range. Just call us at 800 000-0000 or stop by any of our offices.

Sincerely,

---

* Monthly mortgage payments (principal + interest) quoted are based upon a 20% down payment and a conventional 30-year fixed-rate loan at 6.5% with 3 points, A.P.R. 6.795. As an example, a $100,000 loan would mean 360 monthly payments of $632.07. Figures herein do not include property taxes, hazard insurance, or homeowners' association dues for a condominium purchase. Interest rate quoted is as of October 14, 1999, and subject to change.

PROSPECTING - Use a Reader's "To Do" list

Dear

Thank you for your interest in Allied's Model Z-443. As you requested, I have enclosed an application and Disclosure Statement.

If you apply by June 30, you will qualify for a 5% price reduction and several extended benefits which are described in the Disclosure Statement.

<u>To qualify for the 5% discount</u>:

1. Complete the enclosed application.

2. Provide copies of the following:

    *   Architect's drawings, approved
    *   Environmental study, approved

3. Return the completed package to me by June 30.

Call me if you have any questions. You can reach me Monday through Friday between 8:00 a.m. and 4:00 p.m. I am eager to help.

Sincerely,

PROSPECTING - Issue an Invitation

Don't bury information about what-when-where in the body of your letter. If it's important, make it stand out by presenting it like the information on a wedding invitation. Usually the name or kind of event is the most important item, the date and time are the second the most important, and the location the least important. Make it impossible for your reader to miss the information on first reading and easy to retrieve it later.

A Basic Format

Dear

If you feel like it's time for you to take a break and get a fresh look at [subject], you may want to join us at:

NAME OF EVENT
Day of the week, Date
Time
Place

*   Describe a benefit and its accompanying feature.

*   Describe a second benefit and its accompanying feature.

- Describe a third benefit and its accompanying feature.

- Describe a fourth benefit and its accompanying feature.

We've had a lot of [feedback/support/sponsorship] from your [association/office/industry]. With your their/your help and input, we think we can make this event an [exciting/rewarding/fulfilling] experience for everyone involved. A schedule and registration form are enclosed.

Sincerely,

P.S. [Add a *brief* personal appeal.]

An Example

Dear Jack,

If you feel like it's time for you to take a break and get a fresh look at the latest in the world of Esperanto, you may want to join us at:

The 15th Annual
ESPERANTO TRANSLATORS' GETAWAY
Friday/Saturday - October 18-19
Riverview Ranch

Here are just some of the highlights:

- Share the world premiere of the brand new breakthrough *International Esperanto Dictionary* on CD ROM.

- Hear speakers from 11 nations who will update you on the latest advances and developments.

- Meet Dr. David Joranson, who will be discussing <u>New Careers in Esperanto</u>. Several personnel representatives of international corporations will also be present.

- Swim, ride, play tennis, or just loaf. Full spa facilities.

We've had a lot of support from the Northern State Esperanto Association in getting this important event off the ground. With their help and input, we're sure this weekend is going to be a rewarding experience for everyone involved.

Sincerely,

Richard Barthelmess
EVENT ORGANIZER

ENCL: Schedule & reservation forms

P.S. Bob Harron says "Hi," and that he hopes to see you there.

PROSPECTING - Issue an invitation

When Bill Bethel conducted investment seminars, he found this technique very successful. The first invitation was designed to look like a wedding invitation, the same size and shape, and he sent it out hand stamped and addressed. If two weeks went by and the recipient had not replied, Bill followed up with a personal letter which contained two tickets for the seminar. They were imposing tickets, resembling those for important concerts and sports events, and each said the price was $25. Bill wrote:

> Dear
>
> I haven't yet received your R.S.V.P. for the October 16 seminar, *Investing in Your Future*, but I am so eager for you to have the opportunity to be there that I am enclosing two prepaid tickets.
>
> If you find it impossible to attend, please return these tickets to me or pass them on to someone who you feel is as concerned as you are about securing their hard-earned assets against inflation and loss. These tickets are my gift to you.
>
> Sincerely,
>
> Bill Bethel

PROSPECTING - Fund raising

Effective fund raising letters must connect vividly with a genuine motivation in the reader — motivations like pride, patriotism, loyalty, self esteem, hope, or compassion. This poignant real letter uses a case history to put readers in the shoes of people like themselves who suddenly need help.

Dear

        You can imagine the sick feeling you'd have if you left your neighbor's house after a visit and saw thick smoke pouring from the roof of your own house next door.

        That's exactly what Kelly Bradley saw one afternoon. Wide-eyed, heart pounding, she ran home screaming because she'd left her two kids playing a board game in a bedroom.

        The kids had the bedroom door closed and couldn't quite believe the choking smoke that rushed in when Kelly threw the door open and shouted for them to get out of the house!

        They scrambled to safety outside. The roof was disappearing in the leaping flames when Kelly's son remembered Sam, their dog. He'd last seen Sam, old and almost deaf, curled up in his beanbag chair, asleep.

        The Bradleys were in tears when we arrived. Sam had perished in the flames. And the family's home - with all they owned - had been reduced to smoking rubble.

        We couldn't do anything about Sam but gather the family in our arms and wipe away their tears, and then arrange for food and clothing and temporary lodging.

March is Red Cross month. <u>And I hope you'll</u>
<u>give generously to our Annual Fund Drive.</u> Your gift
allows us to help people stunned by tragedy and to
offer other critical Red Cross services. Thank you so
much.

                    Sincerely,

                    Chapter Chairman

P.S. Please give generously to our Annual Fund Drive
       so we can be there to help...and to wipe away
       the tears when tragedy strikes. Thank you.

(Used with permission of Grizzard - the Direct Marketing Agency,
who created this letter to raise funds for the American Red Cross Chapters across the nation.)

PROSPECTING - To people attending a convention

Dear

When you attend the Dingbat Association Conference in San
Francisco next week, Acme Doodads invites you to stop at Booth
22 at the Moscone Center.

We're excited about what our innovative new line of Doodads
could do for your company, and we welcome the chance to show
you in person.

Rod LaRoque and I will be there to demonstrate hot new
applications of our classic *Gizmo*, and to introduce our
Thingamajig which has gotten raves in all the trade papers.

Looking forward to seeing you in San Francisco!

                    Sincerely,

                    Neil Hamilton

P.S.   Bring the enclosed card and we'll swap it
       for a free mini-Gizmo.

PROSPECTING - Resell a past customer

Dear

What's worse than a difficult customer? A dishonest one!

You <u>can</u> foil these chiselers, and do it legally, safely, and confidently. We'll show you how at this special one-day seminar called:

How To Foil the Bad Guys and Have Fun Doing It
(A Step-by-Step Guide)

Learn how to react coolly, confidently, and <u>legally</u> in difficult and dangerous situations.

By now you've had several weeks to apply what you learned at our **Dealing with Difficult Customers** seminar, including stress reduction techniques and specific strategies for handling the key types of tough customers. You've learned how to deal with an "Ida Wannit," a "Rich Switcher" or a "Walk-out Willie" — those frustrating customers with attitude problems that could make your job a miserable chore.

But the most difficult problem that most salespeople face is how to handle a criminal: a shoplifter, a person using a stolen credit card, a bad-check writer, even an armed robber. The salesperson at the counter is the first and last defense against the law breakers that cost our nation billions of dollars yearly, but many are understandably reluctant to take the responsibility.

Read the enclosed brochure for complete details — then call 1-800 000-0000 and reserve a seat at this powerful seminar. Call today, while we still have openings.

Sincerely,

PROSPECTING - Resell a past customer

Dear

Thanks to $5 million worth of renovations last year at our High Mountain Conference Center, we've just completed one of the best ski seasons in our history. Now we're looking ahead to spring, the conference season, and welcoming back our corporate customers.

Is there a conference in your future?

If you inspect our expanded site before June 1 and you book a meeting within 30 days after your visit, we offer the following bonuses:

1. No charge for use of meeting room.
2. Free audio-visual equipment (except video).
3. A complimentary cocktail reception.
4. A complimentary bedroom for every 25 bedrooms occupied.

To qualify for these bonuses, your group must number twenty or more and stay two nights or more.

Why High Mountain is famous:

- 15 restaurants, including 2 award winners
- 15 meeting rooms
- 25 tennis courts
- 2 championship golf courses
- A 20-acre lake
- 1 indoor and 5 outdoor swimming pools
- Children's center
- 25 miles of hiking trails

We are eager to show you how High Mountain Lodge can make your meetings a success, and we're so sure you'll agree that we're making this one-time offer. Please complete the enclosed postage-paid reply card or call me at 1-800 000-0000 for more information.

We look forward to seeing and serving you.

Sincerely,

PROSPECTING - The two-step approach

Plan a double whammy. When you are broaching a really big idea that will take some contemplation, or when you expect resistance, soften your reader up first with an overview, then go back a few days later with the details.

The first letter presents the big idea

Dear

A unique and historic trade conference will take place this December in the People's Republic of China. I would like to extend a formal invitation to you and another member of your firm to be delegates to the *Pacific Rim Trade Technology Conference*. It is sponsored by Trade Programs International under the aegis of the United States State Department.

The delegation will consist of approximately 200 representatives from our industry. It will depart Los Angeles on Saturday, December 7th, and return there on Monday, December 16th. In a few days you will receive more details from Mr. Allan Jones, Vice President of our trade association. In the meantime, if you need any preliminary information, please call me.

Sincerely,

Stanley Smith
PRESIDENT

The follow up asks for a decision

Dear

A few days ago you received a letter from Mr. Stanley Smith regarding your firm's participation the Pacific Rim Trade Conference in the People's Republic of China this December. The purpose of my letter is to provide additional information about the project and the procedures involved in joining the delegation.

[Lots of additional information and supports here.]

Both Mr. Smith and I hope that you can become a member of this project. We look forward to hearing from you.

Sincerely,

Allan Jones
VICE PRESIDENT

PROSPECTING - The two-step approach

Here's a short follow up note to any previous prospecting letter.

Dear

I said you could experience [benefit/feature/product/service] as
you never have before, and I'd like to prove it right now by
inviting you to [describe].

Sincerely,

PROSPECTING - The two-step approach

There are only three kinds of business letters that are almost sure to be
opened and read: those from the IRS, those from a lawyer, and those from
a famous person. Here's a real letter from someone who will probably
catch the reader's attention immediately.

BILL CLINTON

Dear John,

Once again, I need your help.

In 1992, you and I fought for the Presidency on
a platform based on new hope for this country.

And since my inauguration over one year ago, we
have seen the spark of that historic election reignite
the flame of hope in America, and its intensity grows
each day.

But unfortunately, there are many who want to
extinguish that flame simply to further their own
political ambitions.

They only want to see this Administration fail
-- with little, or no, regard for the effects on our
fellow citizens. Their actions threaten to slow, if
not stop, the initiatives that you and I set in motion
in November of 1992.

During the 1992 campaign, as a major leader within our Party, you played a significant role in my election as President of the United States.

Now I must ask you to take the second step in our journey towards progress. I have asked Speaker Foley to contact you concerning a project that is key to the success of this Administration and our initiatives to change this nation.

I urge you to think about what the Speaker has to say, and I hope you'll step forward and help me.

John, ever since I accepted our Party's nomination for President, you've backed me up. And I know I can count on you now.

(Signature)

And the favorably inclined reader looks forward to a second letter from Speaker Foley that will spell out exactly what support is requested.

PROSPECTING - Use the personal touch

Marc Chapdelaine quickly got thirteen positive responses, three more than he needed, to this appeal.

Dear Bill:

As you may or may not know, I worked my way through college as a dinner waiter in a formal hotel dining room.

Because of this vast savoir faire in wait service, I have accepted the opportunity to serve a table of ten at the *7th Annual Celebrity Luncheon for Heart*, a benefit for the American Heart Association of San Mateo County on Friday, March 4th at the San Francisco Airport Hilton, from 11:30 am to 2:00 pm.

This would be your chance to see me serve from the left, clear from the right, and deftly satisfy the requests of the distinguished guests at my table.

This fantastic opportunity is limited to the first 10 guests who RSVP to Margi at 348-0000, x213. In addition to the prompt and courteous service of your waiter, there will be a delicious luncheon and the opportunity to bid on fabulous prizes in a silent auction.

This once-in-a-lifetime opportunity is presented to you at the cost of $30 per person, a portion of which is tax deductible as a charitable donation.

Bill, RSVP today to insure your seat at this prestigious event!

Cordially yours,

Marc Chapdelaine
President / CEO
SAN MATEO COUNTY
CONVENTION & VISITORS BUREAU

(Used with permission of the author, Marc Chapdelaine)

PROSPECTING - Stress exclusivity

Dear

As a past client of Prestige-Plus Motors, you may be interested to know that our marketing firm has been retained to reduce the Prestige-Plus inventory of previously owned luxury vehicles.

More than $2.5 million in recent and classic models will be offered to the public, starting November 10, at their South City facility.

However, we are pleased to inform you that, as a current patron of Prestige-Plus, you may preview these vehicles on <u>Wednesday, November 7</u>. Simply bring this letter with you for admission between 9:00 a.m. and 6:00 p.m. All phone inquiries should be directed to Everett Petherbridge at (000) 000-0000.

Sincerely,

P.S. Naturally, your current relationship with Prestige-Plus entitles you to immediate delivery and on-the-spot credit.

PROSPECTING - Ask for a meeting or interview

Some products and services just can't be sold effectively without personal contact. Your goal is to get your reader to consent to meeting with you or even to talking with you on the phone. Ann Bloch, of *Writing Workout* in Lenox, MA, created this attention-getting letter for a client. It alerts readers to expect a telephone call—if the readers haven't already been moved by the message to call sender first!

Dear

What's wrong with this true story?

> A man inherited a thriving company from his father.
> An accountant, advised by an attorney, set up a trust
> to protect the client's assets from judgments resulting
> from any potential lawsuit. Not only did the client
> thus give up control of his hard-earned assets, he
> found to his dismay that the trust could be penetrated.
> He lost his home and business.

As an accountant, your relationship with clients is based on protecting their assets. In today's volatile business climate—with litigation at an all-time high—you need credible backup you can rely on for unbiased advice. We specialize in advising accountants. We work *with you* to judgment-proof your clients' property. You retain full control over your client relationship.

Our colleague, Attorney Roland Young, has experience as a federal prosecutor in the Tax Division of the Department of Justice. He knows which strategies stand up legally...and which are easily penetrated.

His methods create an impassable legal obstacle in the path of potential judgments.

Read the enclosed fact sheet and resume. I'll call you within several days to discuss the next step to bolster protection for your clients.

Sincerely,

ENCL: Fact sheet and resume

(Used with permission of the author, Ann Bloch)

PROSPECTING - Ask for a meeting or interview

Dear [newspaper manager]

The Allied-Dupe copy system has reduced photocopying costs 15% or more for 8 of the 10 newspapers that have installed our system in the last five years, according to their managers.

May I talk with you for ten minutes to discuss how Allied-Dupe might be able to do the same for XYZ? I'll call Tuesday at 2 PM.

Sincerely,

ENCL: [supports such as endorsement letters, statistics, etc.]

Then be sure that you telephone Tuesday at 2 o'clock!

PROSPECTING - Ask for a meeting or interview

Dear

I will telephone Wednesday at 10:00 AM to ask if I may show you a [name of product] that <u>won't</u> save you money or production time, but which <u>will</u> guarantee an error rate less than .02% — which <u>could</u> save you lots of time, money, frustration, headaches, and customers.

Sincerely,

PROSPECTING - Ask for a meeting or interview

Dear

You probably would like to know how [event, legislation, court decision, etc.] is going to affect you and your [company/ industry], but haven't had the time to research all your options.

Allied has prepared a detailed proposal/analysis based on [respected source such as expert, industry leader, government statistics, etc.]. If you feel this information could be useful to XYZ, we would be happy to share it with you.

Call me at 1-333 000-0000 to arrange a time.

Sincerely,

PROSPECTING - Ask for phone interview

Lee Boyan, author of *Successful Cold Call Selling*, also advocates getting the attention of hard-to-reach prospects by sending a letter in advance of a phone call. "This letter should be short, three paragraphs at most on one page," he advises in his book. "Avoid anything that makes it look like a mass mailing. Call the secretary in advance to check the spelling and if your target will be in the office when your letter and phone call arrive." Here is a pre-call letter that Lee Boyen has found very effective.

Dear

Because of your heavy schedule, I am taking this means to introduce my company and myself.

The enclosed article from *Business News Monthly*, "Are Your Employees Costing You Money...Or Making You Money?" points out dramatically how easily payroll dollars can be wasted. Our firm is currently serving thousands of businesses with a simple and inexpensive supplement to management's efforts. Our clients tell us we have upgraded the performance of their people and reduced their payroll costs substantially.

Perhaps you would like to evaluate our idea in terms of profit for your organization. I will contact you within the next few days for an appointment.

Sincerely,

(Used with permission of the author, Lee Boyen)

PROSPECTING - Ask for phone interview

Dear

If you knew for sure that you could improve your team's sales results by using Bill Bethel's technique, when would you want to talk to Bill to find out how others have benefited?

Did you say "Now"? Then call.

Sincerely,

Bill Bethel

P.S. My number is 1-800 548-8001.

PROSPECTING - Ask for phone interview

Vern Coultrup, an imposing and urbane salesman with stationery to match, developed a contrast technique to capture the attention of potential clients. This forceful, elegant man approached them with almost an "aw, shucks" country boy attitude, asking for their help. Customers were invariably intrigued and complimented because everything about him suggested that he was successful and competent, not anyone who would need their help. Even if you can't match Vern's unique charisma, you can still flatter people by asking for help.

Dear

Maybe you can help me? I think we have a product that could be tremendously useful to you, and I'd like to explain it to you.

Will you give me <u>one minute</u> of your time on the phone next Tuesday at 3:00 o'clock? At the end of that minute, if you haven't heard something useful, you can hang up.

How about it? Will you help me?

Sincerely,

Vern Coultrup

It sounds too simplistic to work, but the number of people who gave Vern his minute was amazing. Naturally Vern was a good talker and few ended the conversation after the first minute.

PROSPECTING - Ask for phone interview

Bill Bethel once got an envelope containing only a business card. On the back was:

[handwritten]

Please call right away.

Eric

The company name gave no clue as to the product or service. Bill strongly suspected this was a clever selling ploy, and resisted for several days. Finally he called and got an expert sales pitch for a service that could save him money — thus the supposed urgency of the message. Bill declined, but with thanks for an example of an effective "sales letter." (Like the empty envelope trick, this works only if no one else is doing it.)

PROSPECTING - Ask for phone interview

Dear

Are your salespeople doing as well as you wish?

Do you think they could do better?

I have an idea that I think will help. Will you give me five minutes to explain it to you? I'll telephone Thursday morning.

Sincerely,

Bill Bethel

P.S. Please ask your secretary to expect me and put me through, okay?

PROSPECTING - FAX for a phone interview

Bill Bethel's FAX FACTS: Keep it short! This FAX nearly always gets him a favorable response.

> Dear
>
> You are a very busy person! I've been unable to get in touch with you. Can you call me Tuesday at my 800 number?
>
> > Bill Bethel

PROSPECTING - FAX for a phone interview

Having exactly what people want is half the battle. Getting them to notice that you do is the other half. René Chlumecky sent the following FAX on his letterhead to 100 target physicians. Two phoned him by 5:00 PM the same day. In total, he got a 19% response.

> Because you are one of the best, your patients chose you.
>
> Wouldn't you like to offer your patients new procedures?
>
> With future health care reimbursement in question, would patient pay procedures benefit your office?
>
> Did you know that preceptorship training for the unique LASER SKIN RESURFACING and LASER BLEPHARPLASTY are available?
>
> Please call 1-800-848-3646 and ask for Mr. René Chlumecky.
>
> (Used with permission of the author, René Chlumecky)

PROSPECTING - Asking for interview when all else fails

Noted sales management trainer Ray Pelletier has only used this letter a few times when he found it impossible to get through to a busy senior executive. He says, "It is incredibly effective, but very risky. Fortunately for me, I have been able to pull it off."

[handwritten]

Phil,
I talked with God this morning. Why
can't I talk to you? Please call.
Ray

(Used with permission of the author, Ray Pelletier)

PROSPECTING - Ask for a reply

Dear

PLEASE! WE NEED YOU!

Why do most business surveys fail so miserably? Because the really important people in the industry are usually too busy to bother filling out questionnaires. The data that results is skewed by responses from folks who aren't as informed and involved. That's right: Garbage in, garbage out.

Please, take one minute to check the opinion boxes on the enclosed Speed Survey and return it in the stamped envelope. (If you wish, you can go on and fill out the longer questionnaire.)

Without your input, the National Trade Association can't anticipate the many challenges we'll all be facing in the next decade. We need your knowledge and ideas so that we can be ready to meet your needs the moment they arise. We don't want to let you down, so please don't let us down.

Please.

Sincerely,

PROSPECTING - Ask for a reply

Always make answering easier than *not* answering. Bill Bethel gets a good response by sending this letter along with a stamped, self-addressed envelope, an "SASE." NOTE: Always use big, colorful stamps on your return envelope. Most people can't stand to waste good postage stamps. They may waffle between soaking off the stamp or throwing it away, and usually end up scribbling a reply, stuffing it in the envelope, and tossing it in their out-box because it's the easiest thing to do.

Dear

You're a very busy woman!

I haven't been able to reach you on the phone, so I'm actually resorting to the post office.

If you would answer the questions below in the blank spaces and return this letter to me in the enclosed stamped envelope, we will both know whether there is a mutual advantage in talking on the phone.

1. Do you ever have a meeting where you hire an outside speaker?

   _____

2. My topics are: Communications Skills, Customer Service, and Sales. (Brochure enclosed.) Do those subjects fit any of your future plans?

   _____

3. If you use outside speakers on these subjects, **what can I do to help you decide to hire me for your next meeting?**

   _____

I believe that my training and experience will make my message unique and valuable to your organization. I would like an opportunity to prove it to you.

Cordially,

Bill Bethel

Enclosure: SASE

PROSPECTING - Ask for a reply

Well-designed reply coupons can save you prospecting and qualifying time, while helping potential customers clarify their needs and options. Here's a two-part reply card created by Stephen P. Duddy for Coherent, Inc. of Palo Alto, CA.

Thank you for your interest in a Coherent Laser. I
enjoyed the opportunity to talk to you
about our products and look forward to speaking
with you again soon.

So that I don't contact you before you're
ready, please take a minute to fill out and return
the reply card below.

_____

[*signature*]

---------------------------------- [fold] ----------------------------------

WHERE DO WE GO FROM HERE?

   ❑   Please call to set up an appointment.
   ❑   Please call. We have additional questions.
   ❑   We are still interested and awaiting approval.
   ❑   Our purchase is on hold.
             Call back: _____
             Contact: _____
   ❑   We've already purchased a laser.
   ❑   We are no longer interested in a laser

_____

(customer's name)

✺ COHERENT.

(Used with permission of the author, Stephen P. Duddy)

PROSPECTING - Ask for letters of recommendation

Every reader is asking, "Can I trust this person?" One way to build trust is to use a third-party recommendation. People like to do what their friends and associates do, and they often trust the people their friends trust. Sometimes they will even believe what a total stranger is saying about you before they'll believe what you are saying about yourself.

If a past customer will give you a letter of recommendation or a testimonial that you can send to your potential customers, that is a very powerful form of third-party influence. Even when your customers won't write a recommendation, often they will let you use their name.

Every time you make a big sale or do something special for your customers, ask them to write a brief letter, describing what benefits they received from your product or service. Use copies of these letters in mailings to similar businesses or people in that geographical area. They constitute an implied recommendation and can open doors.

> Dear
>
> Your Christmas catalogue is a real winner! I'm especially pleased at the role that Allied Delivery could play in rushing them your catalogues to your suburban stores in time for your deadline. We're proud that our extra effort paid off for you.
>
> **If you agree**, when the dust has settled, I'd be grateful if you'd write us a short "testimonial" note that we could use when we tell others about our emergency You-Want-It-When?! Service.
>
> We look forward to the challenge and satisfaction of resolving your next delivery crisis.
>
> Sincerely,

PROSPECTING - Ask for letters of recommendation

> Dear
>
> What do you think?
>
> Back in August, when you were considering ALLIED as your chief supplier, I suggested three reasons we thought we could do the job for you. You agreed.

Have we lived up to our promises? And have you found even more ways that ALLIED has helped XYZ to meet its high professional standards and to fulfill its goals?

If so, could you take a few minutes to write me about XYZ's experiences with ALLIED? I know that we'd be tremendously proud to have your support and to show your recommendation to future clients.

Sincerely,

PROSPECTING - Ask for referrals

Exercise machines are hot right now and NordicTrack makes one of the most popular. They sell mostly by direct marketing or through their own retail dealerships, and count on referrals. Bill Bethel purchased a NordicTrack and received a great follow-up letter that asked for referrals:

Dear Mr. Bethel:

How about you? Are you feeling healthier and stronger lately? More relaxed and more energetic? Congratulations. You've discovered how it pays to get fit and stay fit through total body exercise on your NordicTrack. Now I'd like you to consider sharing your special knowledge with a friend or relative.

....We thank you for your continued support and your friends will thank you for helping with their fitness goals of looking and feeling their best and being the very best they can be.

Sincerely,

(Used with permission of NordicTrack)

A form was provided for submitting referral names and addresses. In addition, NordicTrack owners were offered a less altruistic inducement: a $100 savings bond for every referral who ultimately bought the exercise machine. It was a very effective letter.

PROSPECTING - Ask for referrals

Dear

Please...

IF you've been happy with your Allied Party-Master, and...

IF you know five people who are as eager as you are to offer their guests the finest in homemade pastries, and...

IF you are willing to share their names with us, then...

Allied is eager to show their appreciation by sending you your choice of an eclair-filler attachment or a brioche beater. Just fill out and return the enclosed response card. We'll send them our exciting Fall catalogue, and we'll send you your complimentary pâtisserie tool with our gratitude.

Bon appetit!

Sincerely,

PROSPECTING - Ask for referrals

Dear

You're worth $10 million to us.

That's because your good opinion is our most valuable advertising resource. Forget multi-million dollar TV campaigns and neon-covered dirigibles hanging over sports stadiums. We depend on you.

If you think that Allied did a good job for you and could do the same good job for people you know, we'd like to hear about it. I've enclosed a reply card on which you can write the names and addresses of future Allied boosters. While we can't offer you the $10 million you deserve, we will extend your free maintenance agreement an additional month for each of your referrals who orders from Allied.

Thanks!

DEVELOPING PROSPECTS AND CUSTOMERS

To keep customers, use the same letter skills that go into getting customers. You are "selling" every time you answer a question, respond to a complaint, announce a price change, or explain a delay or cancellation.

DEVELOPING - Answer queries

Here is a format for a typical response letter.

START BY DESCRIBING ENCLOSURES

> Dear
>
> Here is [a brochure/an information package] that should answer most or all of your questions about Allied's [name of product].

OFFER BRIEF SALES PITCH

> We have worked hard to make this [name of product] one of the best in today's tough, competitive market, and we'd like a chance to prove to you firsthand how it can help you and XYZ to [keep ahead of your competition/solve your production problem/speed your deliveries/reduce staff time, etc.].

ADD TRUTHFUL STIMULATOR (if appropriate)

> Our [schedule/calendar/order book] has been filling quickly since [the big convention/article about us in the *Wall Street Journal*/change in regulations], so if you are considering placing an order, we advise early planning.

OR

> If you apply by [date], you'll [be able to/eligible for/can also receive...]

CLOSE ON HOPEFUL NOTE

> Please call me if you would like any additional information. We look forward to being of service to XYZ.
>
> Sincerely,

DEVELOPING - Answer queries

Dear

You asked about our Dual Star triple-press extractor. Here is a copy of our latest catalogue with a full description.

Your offices happen to be fairly near several other manufacturing firms that have installed this system. One especially, Pull-It, Inc. in Eastville, has used two Dual Star extractors for the past five years. You may want to talk to Francis Lederer there about their experiences, both with improved quality control and cost/performance return. A list of contact names and phone numbers is enclosed.

I am also sending you our Production Specifications Manual because you may want a more detailed picture of how the dual valves will interact with your present system.

You can call me at 333 000-0000 when you've had a chance to look over this material. I am eager to answer your questions and to prepare you a savings estimate based on your requirements.

Sincerely,

ENCL: 1999 catalogue
      PSM Manual
      List of purchasers

DEVELOPING - Answer queries

Dear

You'll find the answers to most of your questions, I think, on pages 2, 3, and 17 of the enclosed [document/brochure/article, etc.]. [I have highlighted some passages that may interest you.]

Thank you for taking the time to send us your questions and comments. We depend on people like you and really appreciate your [concerns/interest]. I am sending copies of your letter to our [title, department].

If you have any further questions, I'll be happy to try to answer them. Write me at the above address.

Sincerely,

ENCL: [For example, "Excerpts, 1999 Policy Statement"]

DEVELOPING - Answer queries

Dear

We greatly appreciate XYZ's interest in ALLIED.

Information you requested: The prices you asked for are:

>   Item: $00.00
>   Item: $00.00
>   Item: $00.00
>   Item: $00.00

Analysis of Your Needs: Our consultants will be happy to prepare an assessment of your present and future needs, and to offer specific recommendations for your needs at XYZ.

Some Other Services: ALLIED is constantly working hard to be the leader in our field with the most up-to-date technology available. Did you know that we also offer a wide variety of products/services such as:

- Product/service
- Product/service
- Product/service
- Product/service

Again, thank you for considering ALLIED for your [specify type of] needs. If you have any other questions, please call me.

Sincerely,

P.S. Our consultant, [name], will contact you soon to analyze your needs and to suggest how ALLIED can serve you best.

DEVELOPING - Answer queries

You've undoubtedly seen those pitches for How to Succeed books that tease you with hard-to-believe hooks like these:

```
• Make $1 million a year TAX FREE!  And it's perfectly
legal!  (See page 167)

• From mail room to the board room in just three weeks
— guaranteed!  (See page 387)
```

You can offer a gentle parody of this approach in your cover letter, hooking your readers by citing actual information in enclosed brochures or catalogues.

Dear

Here is your copy of the Allied Spring catalogue with all the top quality produce you've come to expect and rely on, plus some new surprises:

- The fruit that Napoleon fought a war for. (Page 33.)

- What you should never do to a tomato and why. (Page 21.)

- Potatoes can kill you! Find out how and what you can do to keep these tasty tubers trustworthy. (Page 38.)

- Five proven aphrodisiacs for a romantic evening -- and they're legal! (Page 45.)

- What Adam ate before apples: the oldest food known to humanity makes good health sense today. (Page 59.)

We look forward to serving you and your taste buds with the finest, freshest fruits and vegetables on Planet Earth.

Sincerely,

P.S. Attention cherimoya lovers! These delicacies will start arriving from Hawaii shortly. (If you've never sunk your teeth into a cherimoya's succulent yellow-green flesh, check out the recipe on page 91.)

DEVELOPING - Respond to complaints

One angry or unhappy customer is like a ticking time bomb. Numerous surveys indicate that he or she will tell at least a half-dozen people about your failings (real or imagined) and each of those people will mention it to a half-dozen more, and so on. Given human nature and mathematical progressions, your company can get a lot of bad publicity very quickly. MORAL: Keep your customers as happy as possible — or at least impressed with your fairness and concern.

Some writers are eager to deny responsibility for any problem because they fear their company may be sued. However, you can be sympathetic without giving litigious clients real ammunition for a legal battle. Here are the components of an effective response to a complaint. (Some steps may not apply to specific products or services.)

EXPRESS CONCERN that the customer is unhappy (which is not an admission of fault).

> We were very concerned to learn of your experience with our Zip-Master Electric Zipper.
>
> •   •   •
>
> Your report of problems with our DX-40 is of great concern to us.

REACT - Describe what you can and will do to help the customer.

> Please use the enclosed prepaid Express Delivery form to return the parts to me. I will immediately issue you a full credit as soon as they arrive.
>
> •   •   •
>
> We have notified our local representative, Frances Dee, to contact you immediately about repairs or replacement.

DIAGNOSE - Offer a possible explanation (not an excuse) for what happened, if this is appropriate.

> One possibility is that these components were affected by corrosion, due to exposure to salt air. Our Quality Control Lab will conduct exhaustive tests to discover the cause.
>
> •   •   •
>
> Sometimes when the peanut butter comes in contact with especially acidic jam, a chemical reaction occurs that causes a

temporary whitening of the peanut butter. This doesn't affect the taste or quality in any way.

REMEDY - Describe what you can and will do to prevent the problem recurring.

All future shipments to your area will be hermetically sealed and shrink-wrapped to deter contamination.

• • •

Our kitchen experts are currently working on a new peanut butter formulation, testing it with various jams. They want our *Fluffy Nut* to be as much a treat for the eye as it is for the taste buds.

THANK the customer for supporting your organization, as demonstrated by taking the time to report a problem.

Thank you for alerting us to this situation. We greatly appreciate your conscientiousness and depend upon customers like you to help us keep ALLIED the quality leader in the industry.

• • •

Letters like yours are extremely important to us. Your feedback is imperative if we are going to continue to grow and to satisfy your needs.

• • •

We are very grateful to customers like you who take the time to contact us. Your support is greatly appreciated.

REWARD - (Optional) Express your thanks with a coupon, discount, etc.

In the meantime, please accept the enclosed coupon for a complimentary pair of Zip-Master Electric Scissors.

• • •

We invite you to try our newest *Fluffy Nut* Sundae Sprinkles with our compliments. A jar is enclosed.

The following letter starts with concern that the customer *perceives* a problem. This is different from admitting that a problem exists.

Dear

We were concerned to learn of your dissatisfaction with Allied's [name of product].

You said that [repeat complaint]. This [was/may have been] because [explanation]. We have notified our [Director of Quality Control/Shipping Supervisor/District Manager], who will be looking into the situation, [and who may contact you with further questions].

Thank you for the cooperative spirit that prompted you to contact us. Please accept the enclosed adjustment with our apologies. We will try harder to make all your future [Allied purchases/visits to Allied] completely satisfactory.

Sincerely,

DEVELOPING - Respond to complaints

A national business magazine recently featured real examples of good and bad corporate responses to a customer's problem, a shipping delay that had cost the customer a bundle. Even though the "good" letter in the article went a lot further toward soothing the savage breast of the injured customer, we feel it still didn't go far enough.

The writer of the "good" letter cited first made the reader read through three paragraphs -- 175 words -- which list all the reasons, legal and common practice, why the company was not required to help the customer. This included an all-cap statement:

```
ALL POLICIES CURRENTLY WRITTEN BY ANY INSURER
    WILL NOT COVER LOSSES SUSTAINED BY DELAY.
```

Finally, at the bottom of the page in paragraph four, the fuming reader reached the statement that, "We value your business...Therefore, I am offering $0,000..."

How do you think the reader felt at this point? The writer of the original letter certainly didn't intend to alienate a customer. After all, the bottom line (literally) was that the customer was going to be compensated for the loss. Shouldn't that be enough? Well, no.

The "good" example in the article was a typical once-upon-a-time communication that followed the writer's train of thought, but it was still absolutely wrong for the customer-reader. By the time the customer had read through all the reasons why the writer couldn't and wouldn't and shouldn't compensate the customer for the loss, the customer's good will toward the writer's company was probably at rock bottom and his blood pressure sky high. The writer's offer of compensation in the last paragraph comes too late to prevent those feelings.

MORAL: Put what interests your customers first. *Don't* list all the reasons why the law doesn't require you to stand behind your product or service, and *then* say reluctantly that you will make good to keep them as a customer. Start out on the right foot:

> Dear
>
> Here is our credit for $800 to help compensate you for your losses because your February 3 order was delayed in shipping. Even though our insurer refuses to cover any loss due to shipping delays, we know how crucial it is to you to get every Allied shipment on time. That's why we're willing to "eat" this expense. We want to show you how valuable you and your business are to us.

Then, if really necessary, go on to explain any background on the situation, what you are doing to prevent future problems, etc.

DEVELOPING - Respond to complaints

> Dear
>
> Thank you for calling me today about your [billing/service/ shipping, etc.] problem. I understand your frustration and personally apologize on behalf of Allied for the difficulties you had in this situation.
>
> To restate what we agreed, [describe solution.] I hope that this resolution will help to restore your confidence in Allied.
>
> Please consider me your advocate if you have any future problems.
>
> Sincerely,

DEVELOPING - Apologizing

If it's appropriate, a personal apology rather than a corporate one works best. Dottie Walters of Walters International Speakers Bureau believes that a creative, sincere apology can turn a bad situation around and make the sale.

Once, when she was running an ad agency, she arrived for an appointment and found her banker prospect red faced and furious, in the midst of an office crisis. "What the hell do *you* want?" he cried, not recalling his appointment or realizing who she was. Dottie beat a hasty and embarrassed retreat. That night she made some phone calls and got some background on this man. "I learned that he loved a certain type of horse. I found a new book about the breed and had it delivered the next day with this letter."

> Dear
>
> Sometimes things go wrong and wrong and wrong! We all have those terrible moments. Wish I could have done something to help you when I arrived for my appointment with you Tuesday. My heart was with you.
>
> Thought you might enjoy this book. When things calm down and you would like to see me, please call me at 000-0000.
>
> Sincerely,
>
> Dottie Walters
> PRESIDENT

(Used with permission of the author)

Notice that her apology didn't assign blame or accept guilt. How easy it would have been to get mad back and point out this man's rudeness. Instead, she commiserated and gained a customer. He signed a large advertising contract and introduced her to the District Manager. Eventually she signed all this bank's branches in five counties.

DEVELOPING - Keeping customers active

> Dear
>
> Now you get to decide if the new products we've introduced during the past year were worth the enormous effort we made to meet the changing needs in your industry. To be sure you have a chance to find out for yourself, we're offering the following:
>
> > A 20% discount: Just use the enclosed order form to try the newest technology while saving 20%.

<u>And we'll bill you</u>: You don't have to send payment with your order to receive this discount, as long as you use this special order form.

Thanks again for all your support in the past. We'll continue to work hard to bring you the most advanced products, and we're always eager to hear your comments and suggestions.

Sincerely,

DEVELOPING - Announcing price increases

Dear

How can a price increase save you money?

When Allied began manufacturing its famous Turbo-Lamp in 1943, a phone call was a nickel, a gallon of milk was 36¢, and the Turbo-Lamp gave you 400 hours of light for .0010¢ per hour.

Today a phone call costs 20¢ (a 300% increase), a gallon of milk costs $3.08 (a 755% increase) and the Turbo-Lamp now gives you 5,000 hours of light at cost of .0005¢ per hour -- a 50% price <u>decrease</u>!

Allied is enormously proud of the contribution that the Turbo-Lamp has made to the exploration of our planet. We look forward to our challenging role in the forthcoming Mars expedition, and in the colonization of the Solar System.

Sincerely,

DEVELOPING - Announcing price increases

Dear

Did we make the right decision? Your next order will tell us.

When Allied heard about the big price increases in the raw materials that go into our top-of-the-line models, we had a big decision to make:

- Should we maintain our current prices by reducing quality?

- Or should we maintain our quality, even if it meant raising prices?

We didn't agonize for long.   We realized that without our reputation for excellence, we wouldn't keep you as our customer for long. That's why, <u>very reluctantly</u>, we have had to raise our prices 6% across the board.

To take some of the sting out of this move, we are increasing your Preferred Customer discount on quantity orders to 9.5%.

Sincerely,

DEVELOPING - Announcing price increases

Dear

Enclosed is our new price schedule for Spring. We won't try to fool you. Some prices have gone up. But some have gone down.

<u>What Prices Have Gone Up</u>: As you go through the list, you'll see that the increases are principally for products made of wood or for ceramics shipped from Pacific Rim countries.

Quality lumber, as you may know, has nearly doubled in price during the last three years due to more careful harvesting of our precious national forests. Until now, many of our suppliers were able to keep prices down by drawing on their backlog of aging woods. But now the supply is exhausted and they must pass the price increases on to us and to you. The higher ceramic prices reflect larger import duties levied by the U.S. government, plus an increased standard of living for the talented artisans who produce these exquisite pieces.

<u>What Prices Have Gone Down</u>: The news isn't all bad. We're proud that careful purchasing has allowed us to hold the line on our line of fine linens, and an improved warehousing system has cut the handling costs on our extensive collection of quality flatware and kitchenware.

And we are very enthusiastic about our expanded line of exciting party supplies. You can check them out on page 75.

We've eager for your reactions.

Sincerely,

DEVELOPING - Explaining delays and cancellations

Whenever you must let your customers down, tell them as far in advance as possible. A typical delay or cancellation letter would follow this format.

START BY APOLOGIZING

Your order is going to be late and we apologize!

• • •

Your calls to ALLIED have been going unanswered and we apologize!

• • •

Your ALLIED billing has become a victim of computer-age gremlins. We apologize for any inconvenience that you are experiencing!

• • •

We want to apologize for any service delays you may be having, due to Hurricane Griselda.

OFFER SOME COMPENSATION

To get your order to you as quickly as possible, we are shipping it by air at our own expense.

• • •

We are eager to keep you as a customer and will refund your payment for this order. Enclosed is our check for $780.60.

• • •

We will credit your account for $224.05 (our invoice # 831106), plus an additional $50.00 as our thanks to you for staying with us through this difficult time.

• • •

We will reimburse you for any additional expenses you have directly incurred for replacements due to this problem. Just send me photocopies of your bills.

• • •

Will you accept the enclosed vouchers for $100 credit toward future orders?

EXPLAIN PROBLEM (Optional)

As you may be aware, a strike was called against one of our major suppliers by Amalgamated Workers on June 20. Because of this unfortunate dispute, service was suspended from June 23 to July 5 at our Texas plant, delaying shipments two weeks. This means that temporarily we cannot offer our full range of toasters.

• • •

As you may be aware, the recent severe storms along the east coast of the United States have caused numerous delays in air, rail, and trucking shipments. ALLIED is doing everything possible to overcome these delays and restore your services. Our local staff has volunteered to work 80 hours a week during the crisis, and we've flown in sixteen additional workers from other parts of the country.

• • •

Our computer system was designed to serve a customer base of 10,000. That was fine when we started in 1981 with just 30 customers, but, because of the support of people like you, ALLIED has surpassed that capacity. Last October we switched to a system that should serve you well, well into the twenty-first century. Unfortunately, any big change like this can bring tremendously frustrating, if temporary, problems.

EXPLAIN HOW PROBLEM WILL BE SOLVED (Optional)

We are literally working <u>day and night</u> with our supplier to resolve this problem.

• • •

On December 5, our new reactor went on line, which should get us back to normal by next week.

• • •

We expect to restore full service within the next few days.

• • •

Now that the computer problem has been resolved, our warehouse people are working <u>day and night</u> to get your backorders to you. Right now, we anticipate being completely back on schedule by March 12th.

PROVIDE BACKGROUND (Optional)

We would like to give you some background on the disagreement that caused this stop-work action among 20% of ALLIED employees. On January 3 [and here provide a *very* objective, very brief account of the events and management's efforts to resolve the issues, such as: "The Union felt that the scheduling limits set by a federal court could not be implemented in time for the deadline without undue hardship on Union members." *Don't* make anyone out to be the bad guy. Maintain a neutral and regretful tone. Let the reader, if he or she wishes, decide who the real villains are].

CLOSE ON A POSITIVE NOTE

Our biggest concern is to [resolve.../restore service to you/fill your orders] as quickly as possible. Again, we apologize for these problems. Thank you for bearing with us through these difficult days. We value you!

SAYING THANKS

Any time you can sincerely say, "Thank you," do so. Whom should you thank? That's easy. Thank *everyone* — clients, prospective clients, suppliers, colleagues, subordinates, even superiors.

Thank anyone who has done something for you, even if they get paid for it, even if they weren't very good. That's good etiquette.

Thank anyone who has done something extra or outstanding, even if it was "just my job." That's good business.

Praise excellence and acknowledge effort. Personalize. There are few things more devastating than laboring mightily and then getting a terse, impersonal thank-you form letter.

Mention what the reader did and describe your reaction. If you weren't there, describe what you have heard about it. If you heard only bad things, describe how important the job was and how you appreciate that it was done. Ignore your parents' adage that if you can't say something nice, don't say anything at all. Good or bad, a creative writer can find something positive to say about any event.

Warm, sincere, personal thank you letters offer a higher eventual return than any other sales letter! (But *never* begin a thank you letter with the unfortunately common phrase: "I just wanted to take a moment to thank you for ..." Although you don't mean it that way, it's insulting, implying that a moment is all the reader is worth.)

SAYING THANKS - For interview

Dear Gerda,

I would like to thank you again for your time today and your enthusiasm about putting the Allied Tracking Technology Program to work for XYZ. I am preparing a proposal and contract to your specifications, and they should be ready within a few days.

Stan, I know you have to get approval of your partners to institute this system at XYZ. If they express any reluctance to move forward with Allied, please stress that since the payback is so extraordinary, it's a move that makes good economic sense.

When you talk to Franco and Jill, you can emphasize that:

• A year from now at the very latest, according to your own calculations, you will have recovered your investment and have a system that will serve you for many years to come.

• Three hundred local firms now use the Allied system.

• Allied has the financial strength and stability to maintain ongoing research and development. We were number 25 on Forbes' 1999 list of the top 200 small companies, based on financial analysis.

• Only Allied designs, manufactures, tests, markets, installs, and supports all of its products directly. We offer the state of the art in the industry.

We look forward to a productive partnership with XYZ. I'm eager to answer any further questions and to assist you in your "selling" efforts.

Sincerely,

SAYING THANKS - For interview

Dear

It was very rewarding to meet with you yesterday, and to go over your needs and challenges. Your whole operation is tremendously impressive.

I'm enclosing the follow-up material about [describe] that we discussed. You'll hear from me in a few days, in case you have thought of any new questions or have had some new perspectives.

Please tell [name] that I appreciated the [valuable background/tour of your facilities/driving instructions, etc.].

Sincerely,

Enclosures: [List them!]

SAYING THANKS - For interview

Dear

It was a genuine pleasure meeting you yesterday and getting to know the specific needs and issues that apply to XYZ's long-term requirements.

Some important ways that Allied can help XYZ reach those goals are:

Our full-service research department: We can respond to your short-term and long-term research needs more economically than you can in-house, while guaranteeing you full proprietary control over results.

Our full marketing and promotional services: Allied's promotional people, the tops in their field, are available to you on an as-needed basis, but you pay only for time plus materials, not the commission usually charged by outside organizations.

Our site-planning resources: Allied currently manages 12 million square-feet of prime real estate in the area, and represents landlords of another 40 million square-feet. As XYZ's needs change, you will have immediate access to a substantial number of existing and planned sites for your consideration.

Thank you for meeting with us. We look forward to putting Allied's resources to work for you and XYZ.

Sincerely,

SAYING THANKS - For interview

Dear

Your tooling problems are certainly complex, and I was impressed with how you are handling them in a creative and systematic way.

The more I have thought about your concerns, the more I am certain that the #245 model of the Alliedyne System could solve many of the problems you mentioned and still keep your monthly overhead costs at their current level. This would free you up to spend more time in the Design Lab.

Call me any morning at 1-333 000-0000 if you'd like me to explain how this would work for you.

Sincerely,

SAYING THANKS - For contact at convention

Dear

Thank you for visiting our booth at last month's STATE EXPO. The show was quite successful, with an overwhelming response to our new product introductions. [You can add comments about reader's interests or questions here.]

To recap ALLIED's newest products for you:

- Benefit A because of Feature A.
- Benefit B because of Feature B.
- Benefit C because of Feature C.

● Benefit D because of Feature D.

We appreciate your interest at the show and look forward to discussing these innovative ideas with you in the future.

Sincerely,

P.S. [Name] will call you soon about the [name of product that might interest prospect.]

SAYING THANKS - For referral or recommendation

Dear

Thanks for your [valuable referrals/glowing recommendation]. I'm very grateful for your support and your confidence in Allied. We are always pushing to do the best for our customers, and we're proud that you are one of them.

Sincerely,

SAYING THANKS - For your business

Dear

You and I weren't born yet when Joshua Fisher started Allied sixty years ago. Even so, I'm grateful to him and the little tool business he set up in his barn, using a $300 loan from his skeptical father-in-law.

I'm glad he did. If he hadn't, I wouldn't have had the pleasure of working with you over the past two years. Without your support and confidence, Allied would still be back in the barn.

Thanks for being our customer and getting us out of the hayloft.

Sincerely,

P.S. He paid the loan back in four months.

SAYING THANKS - For your business

Dear

Thank you.

We're proud that we can count you among our long-time clients. Whenever this pressure-cooker business of ours starts to get to me and I find myself muttering, "What the heck am I doing this for, anyway?" — then I glance at my phone directory, and I'm reminded of the excitement and satisfaction of working with great people like you every day. You make every ringing phone a fascinating challenge and a new adventure. In short, you make life <u>fun</u>.

Thank you.

SAYING THANKS - For your business

Dear

Five years ago we were working out of our garage, but you had faith in us and what we were trying to do. Today we have our own plant and three outlets, and you're still with us.

We couldn't have done it without your support. <u>Thanks for being our customer</u>!

Sincerely,

SAYING THANKS - Welcome to a new customer

Dear

It is my great pleasure to welcome you as a new Allied purchaser. We look forward to serving you for many years to come.

Your [documentation/*Introduction to Allied* booklet/first statement/membership card] is enclosed.

<u>Some features</u> that may be especially [useful/interesting/ important] to you as a new customer are:

- [benefit/feature]

- [benefit/feature]

- [benefit/feature]

If I can ever be of assistance, please call me toll-free at
1-800 000-0000.

Cordially,

SAYING THANKS - Welcome to a new customer

Dear

Welcome to FAST-AIR, and thank you for requesting this Air
Starter Kit.

Shipping Kit enclosed: You'll find everything you need to start
shipping today and saving right away. Your FAST-AIR account
number is 0000000000. For your convenience, a card with your
account number is also enclosed.

Be sure to notice two very important FAST-AIR guarantees:

1. **Refund guarantee**: However you send your shipment
    (FAST-AIR Next Day Air, FAST-AIR 2nd Day Air, or
    FAST-AIR 3 Day Select), if your shipment is not delivered
    by the time we promise, we'll refund the shipping charges.

2. **24-hour hot line tracking**: Whenever you call our 24-hour
    tracking hot line to check on a shipment's tracking status,
    we'll have your answer in seconds. If we ever take longer
    than 30 minutes, we'll refund the shipping charges.

In choosing FAST-AIR, you've made an important decision for
your business. Our on-time delivery record and our money-back
guarantees are second to none.

Toll-free help line: if you ever have any questions about shipping via FAST-AIR (like the latest pickup time in your local area) just call our toll-free help line: 1-800-FAST-AIR.

Again, welcome. And thank you for using FAST-AIR.

Sincerely,

P.S.   As I mentioned in my initial letter, after you send your first FAST-AIR shipment, we'll send you a free FAST-AIR telephone speed-dialer already programmed with 1-800-FAST-AIR — just to remind you how easy it is to use FAST-AIR.

SAYING THANKS - For a good job

Dear Bill,

Your appearance at our Annual Convention was a big hit.

Your information was great! You gave our people a fantastic presentation that presented solid training in a highly entertaining package. You seemed to be completely at ease, despite the technical problems with the hotel audio system, and you made an outstanding impression.

I'm looking forward to another program with you in the future.

Thank you again, very much.

Best regards,

SAYING THANKS - When it's hard to do

What about a thank you letter when there isn't much to thank? Imagine another convention speaker named Sam who tried hard but was really quite a flop. He was poorly organized, sweated profusely, miscued his slides, and lost his place several times. People dozed off and some walked out. It's still essential to acknowledge poor Sam's effort (which was probably considerably greater than Bill's). Here's how a skilled writer might respond to Sam:

Dear Sam,

We are grateful for the considerable time and expertise that went into your special presentation for our Annual Convention. It was greatly appreciated.

We can't hear your important message too often, and you gave our people much to think about in the months ahead. Your energy in the face of technical problems was admirable, especially in the difficult after-lunch time slot.

Accept our gratitude for your hard work and dedication.

Thank you again, very much.

Best regards,

(The above letter is appropriate for a one-time effort that went wrong. Of course, if you are the supervisor or good friend of someone like Sam, and Sam is going to have to keep doing whatever he did so badly, you will want to go on to counsel him about improving his performance.)

SAYING THANKS - A checklist form

If there are a lot of people you need to thank—for example, after a big job, convention, presentation, major campaign, etc.— or on a hectic sales call schedule, or if it's hard to keep your thank you's sounding fresh and sincere, here are some ideas to start your creative juices flowing.

Postcards (discussed on page 64) are great for quick thank you's. Keep a stock, already stamped, in drawer and briefcase.

You could also make up a Thank You Checklist of possible responses. Whenever you spot someone you could or should thank—as you go through your mail, after a phone call, or immediately following sales calls, conventions, conferences, important meetings, etc.—jot the person's name at the top of your form, check off the appropriate boxes and fill in the blanks. Later you or your secretary can quickly craft these checklists into much appreciated thank you notes or letters.

On the following page is a *Sample Thank You Checklist* to spark your thining. You could make up a similar check list customized to your own needs and clients.

SAMPLE THANK YOU CHECKLIST

Dear _____

Thanks so much for

       ☐ helping with ...
       ☐ participating in ...
       ☐ contributing to ...
       ☐ taking the time to ...
       ☐ backing us up on ...
       ☐ your extra effort to ...
       ☐ meeting our deadline for ...
       ☐ helping to make the project a big success.
       ☐ being such an important part of the winning team.

We / I really appreciate your

       ☐ hard work.
       ☐ extra effort.
       ☐ valuable contribution.
       ☐ taking time from your busy schedule.
       ☐ bailing us out when ...
       ☐ always being there for us.
       ☐ valuable input and insights.
       ☐ unfailing support and encouragement.
       ☐ composure and cheerfulness when the going got rough.
       ☐ commitment and concern. No one could have worked harder.

You certainly

       ☐ increased my awareness of ...
       ☐ expanded my view of ...
       ☐ met all the difficulties with energy/a cool head/
             a real understanding of the problems involved.
       ☐ were wonderful, terrific, and definitely on target.

(AND A CLOSING)

☐ It was a great success, and we couldn't have done it without you.
☐ Everything went even better than I had dared to hope for.
☐ It was everything I hoped it would be.
☐ Thanks for helping to make the project such a success.
☐ Thanks for helping to bring it all together.
☐ We look forward to working with you again.
☐ On behalf of ALLIED, my sincere appreciation for a job well done.

Sincerely,

CONGRATULATIONS

People love to be noticed when something they've done deserves favorable comment. It shows you care and that they are important. A genuine letter of congratulations is worth more than all the advertising, direct mail brochures, and fancy attention-getters. It proves you recognize individuals and their accomplishments.

CONGRATULATIONS - On published article

Dear Gene,

Your article in the December issue of the *G.A.S.P. Journal* was great. I'm not sure which I appreciated more — your insight into the problems of our industry or your lively writing style.

Gene, all of us at G.A.S.P. owe a lot to you and the other members who take the time to keep our industry in the forefront. Thanks for contributing and being such an enthusiastic booster.

Sincerely,

P.S. Your ideas about exports were on-target and tremendously helpful.

CONGRATULATIONS - On new job

Dear

I was delighted to read in the Wall Street Journal yesterday that you are now with the XYZ Corporation.

What a triumph for them to get you! But they have a reputation for attracting the best people, and I'm confident you'll soon eclipse anything done by your celebrated predecessors.

Congratulations!

Cordially,

CONGRATULATIONS - On promotion

Dear

I just heard that you've been promoted! Mazel tov, félicitations, and yahoo! Allied couldn't have made a better choice.

It will be a pleasure to know that our account is in such capable hands.

Best wishes,

CONGRATULATIONS - On retirement

Dear

Where has the time gone! It seems incredible that you're eligible to take retirement already.

How strange it's going to be, not hearing your cheery voice and wonderful laugh on the other end of the phone, but I'll keep thinking of you and Pat in your new roles as horse breeders and devoted grandparents. I look forward to getting snapshots of your progeny, both the two-footed and four-footed varieties.

We'll really miss you!

MAKING ANNOUNCEMENTS

Something is happening. Something is different. Unless you're trying to keep it as quiet as possible, make it easy for your readers to get the news from *their* point of view. Figure out what they need to know and what they want to know. Put that information center stage, down at the footlights. Then throw a big spotlight on it.

MAKING ANNOUNCEMENTS - Of a name change

Dear

We've got a new name and we want to tell you why.

Because your business is important to us, we're changing — changing our focus, our customer support network, and our

<u>name</u>. You may have read, seen, or heard:

H & A PRODUCTS is now *SUPER-ALLIED*.

We know you've come to rely on the name of H & A PRODUCTS over the years, so it was a big step for us to change such a trusted name.

But we're convinced that we've outgrown the H & A label, and that the exciting new services and expanded technologies we're going to be offering deserve an exciting new name. We're still the same dependable company, but our future emphasis will be on moving all of us into the twenty-first century.

Super New Services from *SUPER-ALLIED* include:

• **Super One-Stop Analysis** of your individual challenges in the marketplace of the year 2000, including personal tips from top industry experts, all through *SUPER-ALLIED*.

• **Super Access** to the most distinguished vendors and advanced technology.

• **Super Service** customized to match your changing needs in a dynamic industry.

Questions? During the coming year, you'll be hearing more about our new combinations of products and services. Of course, if you have any questions now about what the new *SUPER-ALLIED* means to your business -- or any suggestions for changes you'd like to see -- please feel free to call us at 1-800 000-0000.

Thank you for offering us this opportunity to be an even greater resource for you and XYZ.

Sincerely,

NOTE: Also take a look at the before and after versions of name a change letter announcement on pages 62-64.

MAKING ANNOUNCEMENTS - Of a change of policy

Change is good. Maybe. If your customers aren't surprised, confused, inconvenienced, or convinced that you're trying to put something over on them. Announce changes very clearly. Spell them out. Be sure you've got your reader's attention. (Before you mutter about "those @#* people who don't read their mail," think about all the announcements and notices you've gotten and didn't read until it was too late.)

IMPORTANT NOTICE

YOU MUST CHOOSE ONE OF THREE OPTIONS.

Dear

You are currently enrolled in Sky-Dish's Optional Maintenance Plan. For a standard monthly fee, it covers repairs and replacement of all parts and cables, at no additional cost to you.

Beginning June 1, the price of this plan will increase from $.75 to $.95 per month. The increase will appear in your July bill, retroactive to June 1st.

You have three options:

1. Keep the Optional Sky-Dish Maintenance Plan you currently have. If this is your choice, don't do anything. We'll simply bill you at the new rate of $.95 per month.

2. Upgrade to our Sky-Dish Enhanced Maintenance Service for just $2.00 a month. Complete details are in the enclosed brochure. To subscribe, call toll-free 1-800 000-0000.

3. Discontinue your current plan at no charge. To discontinue, call toll-free, 1-800 000-0000.

Please read the enclosed information carefully, including terms and conditions. Whatever your choice, we are happy to serve you.

Sincerely,

MAKING ANNOUNCEMENTS - Of a new policy

Dear

CHANGE IN BILLING PROCEDURES

Starting March 15, Allied will begin charging a 5% monthly carrying fee on all balances more than 60 days past due.

We have been very reluctant to take this step, especially since many of our accounts have been with us for quite a few years. All of us been through good and bad economic times together, so it was especially difficult for us to decide to make this change.

As always, we are very willing to work with our clients whenever problems arise.

Sincerely,

MAKING ANNOUNCEMENTS - Of a new policy

NOTICE:

CHANGE IN TRADE-IN POLICY

Dear

Starting February 15th, the items that Allied can accept as trade-ins for recycling will change as follows:

NO LONGER ACCEPTED
- Model C101-B
- Model X133-Z
- Model Y222

STILL ACCEPTED
- All Model B101's
- All jet models

We deeply regret any inconvenience this change will cause you. Unfortunately, the recycler we have used for the past ten years is no longer able to accept these parts at his current location. He is seeking new facilities and also exploring new processes to render these parts ecologically harmless.

If we are able to make new arrangements, we will let you know immediately. In the meantime, we apologize. We felt really good about being able to offer this valuable service, and hope we can do so again.

Sincerely,

MAKING ANNOUNCEMENTS - Of an event

Dear

The Association of Personnel Managers and the Mediators' Society are pleased to announce a jointly sponsored free workshop on one of the most critical issues facing us today:

CONFLICT RESOLUTION IN THE WORKPLACE

Wednesday , April 4

7:00 to 9:00 p.m.

Hotel West Port

Topics will include:

- How to mediate without being caught in the crossfire

- Interdepartmental rivalry — good or bad?

- When healthy ambition steps over the line

- The dangerous employee — When do you step in?

Reply by Friday, March 31 if you plan to attend. Please return the enclosed card to Bob Simpson or me, or call us.

We look forward to seeing you there.

Sincerely,

MAKING ANNOUNCEMENTS - Of personnel changes

Dear

Here are six Roladex cards that will bring you up to date on the recent personnel shifts here at Allied.

We've had a lot of changes. George Formby, our New Products Director for the past eleven years, is retiring, as of June 5th, and Jack Hulbert will be taking over that department. To replace Jack, Jessie Matthews is stepping up to Plastic Lab Manager, and her long-time assistant, Cecily Courtneidge, will ably fill her shoes in Production. Our new Lab Coordinator is an enterprising (relative) youngster, Evelyn Laye, who has spent the last eight years as a V.P. with J. B. Cochran Products.

Since you can't tell the players without a score card, we've listed everyone's new titles and extensions on the enclosed phone directory cards. Just snap the cards in place and give us a call.

Sincerely,

MAKING ANNOUNCEMENTS - Of personnel changes

Dear

Ezra Winslow has left Langdon, Keaton, Chaplin, and Chase as of November 16th, and is no longer a partner with our firm.

[If Mr. Winslow has left under a cloud, you needn't say any more. Otherwise, provide some reason, such as ill health, or his decision to join a monastery or keep bees. If he has gone to another firm, be sure to say so with as much or as little enthusiasm and thanks as you deem necessary.]

Mr. Winslow's accounts are being assigned to the remaining partners, and you will hear from either Mr. Keaton or myself within a few days, to make the transition as seamless as possible. We look forward to a continuing and productive collaboration.

Sincerely,

MAKING ANNOUNCEMENTS - Of a death

Dear

It is with great regret that we announce the sudden death on April 21 of Rosa Chan, a valued and highly esteemed colleague here at ALLIED.

Ms. Chan has been Chief Auditor in our Wichita office for the past four years. Her cheerfulness, energy, and skill will be sorely missed by her many friends here at ALLIED and in the business community.

For the time being, Ms. Chan's duties will be taken over by Denis Ducastel, Assistant to the President. Please direct your inquiries to Mr. Ducastel at ext. 808.

Sincerely,

SAYING "NO" NICELY

Prospects and clients want business concessions, personal favors, and your attendance at various functions. A refusal could be seen as a rejection, souring the business relationship, but you can't possibly say "yes" to every request. The secret is to say "no" in a way that leaves the requester feeling good without holding out false hope.

Obviously, you'll need to say why (tactfully) when you turn anyone down for credit or promotion. Some experts also recommend offering reasons (excuses) when you decline invitations or requests. I disagree with that. This leaves you open to argument, and readers may feel insulted, seeing it as an "either/or" situation: "If you weren't donating to that charity or attending that event, then you would donate to *my* charity or attend *my* event." Quite naturally they will be certain that their own interests are much more pressing and worthy than anything you've chosen instead. It doesn't matter that you'd rather have root canal surgery than sit through their luncheon. Don't tell them that. Just say "no" nicely, firmly, and *usually* without excuses.

SAYING "NO" NICELY - Refusing donation

Dear

Your interest in [health services for the elderly/music for inner city children/an international cooperation program] is admirable, and I am impressed with XYZ's commitment to this important aspect of our community. Your willingness to sponsor and support this valuable resource is inspiring.

Although Allied isn't able to offer a donation right now or in the near future, we applaud your efforts and the importance of your work. You certainly deserve to get the funding you need to [continue/expand] your current operations. Keep up the great job!

Sincerely,

SAYING "NO" NICELY - Refusing invitation

Dear

I am still glowing with surprise and pleasure that you would ask me to [join your organization/speak at your luncheon/permit you to use my name as a referral, etc.]. My initial pleasure makes me all the more unhappy because I won't be able to accept your [kind offer/gracious invitation/intriguing challenge/fine tribute, etc.].

But thank you so much for asking me. I appreciate [your thoughtfulness/your confidence/the honor/the compliment.]

Cordially,

SAYING "NO" NICELY - Refusing invitation

Dear

It was tremendously [kind/flattering/gracious] of you to think of me in connection with your Awards Banquet. I regret that I won't be able to attend, but it is certainly [heartwarming/encouraging/ inspiring] to know that so many people are [supporting this fine work/enthusiastic about advancing this important cause/ remembering the important contributions of this leader in our industry].

My best wishes for a very successful event.

Sincerely,

SAYING "NO" NICELY - Refusing credit

Dear

Your enthusiasm for Allied's new Roto-Auto, demonstrated by your May 11 order, is very encouraging to us. We're proud of this innovative product and think you'll get an excellent response from your customers.

At the moment, we do not yet have enough credit information on file to let us ship your order without prepayment. You can call Marie-Noëlle Foulatier at ext. 845 or fill out and return the enclosed application form.

[OR: I've gone over your application and tried hard to find a way to add XYZ to our list of credit customers, but right now, with the information I have, I just can't see a way to do it.]

As a temporary measure, we can ship your order immediately when we receive your check for full payment which is $19,943.66. I am looking forward to working with you.

Sincerely,

COMPLAINING

If your letters of complaint don't get the results you'd like, here's a technique for producing effective, problem-solving letters.

When you are really angry, *write*! Don't phone. Don't FAX. Don't use E-Mail or computer bulletin boards. *Write* what you want to say on a sheet of paper or in a word processor file. Then close the file or set the page aside. "The quickness of response available with E-mail may lead to *flaming*," wrote Robert Kelley in the June 1987 *PC Week*, "where people impulsively react to a message and send uncensored, emotionally laden and often derogatory return messages — a practice that is almost non-existent in paper writing."

We are never so eloquent as when we are furious. Flame away. Identify the villains and their outrageous conduct. List all the reasons for your anger. Be as furious, sarcastic, petty, rude, or obscene as you wish. Fill page after page. You can say anything you want because *no one will ever see these words but you!*

Then, after an appropriate breather, start again and write at the top of the page:

"What I want to be different after the reader reads this letter."

Go back to your angry pages and underline everything your reader needs to know if you are going to achieve the result you want. Discard the rest. What's left is the first draft of your actual letter.

You probably felt a lot better after writing your original version. How will your reader probably feel after reading your edited version? Is this how you want him or her to feel? Is your anger directed at the right person? Will the reader be more cooperative and eager to help you after getting your letter? Will your edited version produce the results that you want? Refine your letter until it is a tool for productive change.

A Basic format

Dear

I need to know <u>immediately</u> what you will do to prevent any more recurrences of the problems that we have been having with your [describe].

<u>Problems</u>

- [Describe, including date and time if relevant]

- [Describe, including date and time if relevant]

Background [If applicable, offer history of problem or supports and proofs of any damages caused by this problem.]

What I Want You to Do

1. By [set a time and date] [then describe exactly what you want to happen or stop happening, and offer a suggestion for a temporary emergency solution].

2. [Ask reader to provide a permanent solution, perhaps through a change in procedures or a meeting with XYZ officials.]

3. By [date], report to me exactly what steps you have taken and what additional help we can offer to see that this never happens again.

I'm confident that you'll come up with a practical solution. We are eager to work with you so that this will won't recur.

Sincerely,

COMPLAINING - To a customer

Dear Jess,

I need to know immediately what you will do to prevent any more refusals by your XYZ *Captain Cod* franchises to accept our deliveries of frozen fish. You will appreciate that these refusals put Allied in an impossible situation and must be resolved at once.

Problem

- On May 2, James Dunn, manager of your Glen Ellyn *Captain Cod* franchise, refused to accept delivery of your P.O. #29873, our Invoice B-296, for 2,000 lbs. of assorted frozen fillets. He said that his computerized receiving forms from XYZ did not acknowledge the order. Allied's refrigerated truck had to return the fish 280 miles to the Allied Freezer Plant in Riverwood, costing Allied approximately $410 in lost time and trucking charges, as well as delaying other deliveries.

• Similarly, on May 11, Carol Takamura, owner of three Neewollah *Captain Cod* stores, refused our delivery of your P.O. #30117, our Invoice B-771, for 4,300 lbs. of cod fillets and 500 lbs. of shrimp. She said that your computerized receiving forms specified 4,300 lbs. of shrimp and 500 pounds of cod for delivery on June 11, so she could not accept delivery. This refusal tied up one of our trucks for 2-1/2 days, and we had to rent 2 additional trucks to make our regular deliveries.

• Yesterday, our truck with 6,100 lbs. of clams (your P.O. #34274, our Invoice B-882) was not allowed to unload at your North Laurel store by manager Ben Turpin. Currently that order is still on the truck, which is making other deliveries in the state and which will return to North Laurel in four days.

Background: Jess, back on March 18, I alerted you to our ongoing delivery problems and you promised that your new Head of Shipping was going to straighten everything out. I think we've been more than patient.

What I Want You To Do

1. By Tuesday, May 21 at the latest, instruct Ben Turpin at your North Laurel store to accept delivery of your P.O. #34274, our Invoice B-882, when our driver returns.

2. Set up a system of emergency telephone authorization for deliveries. This way our drivers can have your franchises phone you on the spot for special authorization if the need arises.

3. By Friday, May 24 at the latest, report to me exactly what steps you have taken and what additional help Allied can offer to see that this never happens again.

You don't like these snafus any more than we do, I know, and I'm confident that you'll come up with a practical solution. We are eager to work with you so that this will never happen again.

Sincerely,

COMPLAINING - To a supplier

Dear Ms. Roy:

I need to know <u>immediately</u> what you will do to prevent the unacceptable rate of failures of your Z-2000 diodes. Our contract allows a tolerance of 2,000 hours with a failure rate of .05%, but the failure rate has averaged more than three times that for some shipments.

<u>Problems</u>: Jack Carson's data on failure rates is enclosed.

<u>Background</u>: We met with Arthur Jefferson, Stan Laurel, Eve Arden, and you at XYZ on November 4 and again on January 10 to try to resolve this problem. Our notes from that meeting are enclosed.

<u>What I Want You To Do</u>

    1. Immediately authorize our return of our current stock of 8,000 gross of Z-2000 diodes for full credit. (Copies of invoices and purchase orders enclosed.)

    2. Immediately ship us 8,000 gross of Z-4000 diodes. We request that these be billed to us at the lower Z-2000 rate.

    3. By February 15, let me know exactly what steps you have taken and what guarantees you are able to make that your Z-2000 diodes will meet specifications in the future.

I'm optimistic that you'll be able to resolve this. We are eager to work with you and XYZ, but this rate of failures is totally unacceptable.

Sincerely,

CULTIVATING AND FOLLOW UPS

Once you have developed a prospect or acquired a customer, don't let the contact cool. When you sit down each day to generate Bill Bethel's *Magic Five* letters and notes, be sure to cultivate and follow up to generate goodwill for future sales.

CULTIVATING AND FOLLOW UPS - Ticklers

"Ticklers" are any letters or notes that are sent to keep communication open and to remind people of your existence and interest. The simplest might look like this:

Dear

Haven't talked to you for some time and thought I'd just say, "Hello, can I be of service?"

Best wishes,

•   •   •

Dear

You immediately came to mind when I read about [the trade agreement/the terrible floods/the Supreme Court decision/XYZ's exciting new patent]. How are you [doing/handling it/holding up/celebrating]?

Sincerely,

•   •   •

Dear

When I looked at the calendar this morning, I immediately thought of you.

A year ago this week, we were in the midst of [installing your new system/closing on your house/stamping out fires together at XYZ/reveling over your triumph/commiserating over your setback/trying to imagine the end of this project].

What a [difficult/exciting/rewarding/challenging] time! How are things going for you now?

Cordially,

CULTIVATING - Tickler postcards

Ticklers can be service pieces, offering market news or helpful information without any direct references to buying something. Some people even send regular newsletters.

Bill Bethel sends out an "Idea of the Month" printed on an oversized postcard to his client and prospect list.

IDEA OF THE MONTH

BILL BETHEL ON *"CLEAR COMMUNICATION"*

During World War II, the U.S. Office of Civil Defense issued these instructions: *Such preparations shall be made as will completely obscure all buildings during an air raid for any period of time from visibility by reason of internal or external illumination. Such obscuration may be obtained either by blackout construction or by termination of the illumination.*

President Franklin D. Roosevelt changed this to: *During air raids, either cover the windows or turn out the lights.*

Keep your messages short and simple:

1. Use plain, powerful vocabulary.
2. Use action verbs: *"Go,"* rather than *"Someone should go."*
3. Cut every unnecessary word. Remember *KISS* — Keep It Short & Simple.

NEXT MONTH: SHEILA MURRAY BETHEL ON LEADERSHIP

(Reduced 50 percent)

CULTIVATING - Personalized tickler cards

Stu Heinecke Creative Services in Seattle sells a line of ten different customizable cards on computer disk in a Personal Promotion Kit. The idea is that you show prospects how important they are as individuals, and you do it with humor. Stu says he personally tested the concept on 1,300 prospects and got 1,300 appointments.

"The only problem," warns Heinecke, "is that some people say 'What a great idea!' They try to copy our format, but they don't realize that it's very easy to insult someone when you're trying to be funny. Then they end up making enemies."

Here's an example of Heinecke's on-target humor, sent to Bill Bethel. "Almost no one throws these cards away," says Heinecke. "Even if the VIP doesn't bite right away, secretaries *love* cartoons about their bosses, so these cards often stay tacked up on the wall, keeping you in their minds." (This is a good reason to have your name and address on the back of the cartoon, in case it is cut away from the facing page.)

"Have you seen the latest issue of the Journal? It's all 'Bill Bethel this, Bill Bethel that' and nothing about us."

(Used with permission of Stu Heinecke Creative Services)

CULTIVATING - Retaining customers

Dear

Your membership expires <u>this month</u>.

<u>Advantages of renewing immediately</u>:

> • Uninterrupted access to our two 4-star downtown locations, just a few steps from your office, with complete gym and spa facilities including our new lava-rock steam room and jai alai courts. Open 6 A.M. to midnight weekdays.

> • Renewed energy, weight maintenance, body tone, and vigor.

> • The exciting menu at Members Only, our vegetarian Health Bar that gives new meaning to "Power Lunch." Will you ever forget Helga's award-winning cole slaw? And Helga's homemade carrot cake is irresistible.

<u>Disadvantages of renewing immediately</u>: Helga's homemade carrot cake is irresistible.

Think about it.

Sincerely,

CULTIVATING - Recapturing former or inactive customers

Dear

You haven't used our [services/product] for a long time. Is there a problem that we should know about?

Your business is very important to us, so we want to be sure that we have lived up to your expectations.

<u>Please</u> let us know how we can serve you better. I've enclosed a reply card for your comments. I look forward to hearing from you and to being of service in the future.

Sincerely,

ENCL: Reply card

CULTIVATING - Recapturing former or inactive customers

The Executive Speechwriter Newsletter
Emerson Falls Business Park • St. Johnsbury • Vermont • 05819 • U.S.A. • 802/748-4472

Dear "Former" (I **hate** that word) Subscriber:

Months and months ago we first embarked on a meaningful relationship. Now the party's over.

Or is it?

If you already miss us and all that great material that somebody else is using right now, here's one more chance to reclaim "Podium Power" by re-subscribing to the Number One source of speechmaking and speech writing materials and services.

You see, we want **you** to have the best material, not your competitor. We want **you** to have the best stories and quotes, not your competitor. And we want **you** to have the best jokes and one-liners, not the...you get the message.

Not persuasive enough? Then ruminate on this: In an intensely competitive world:

One great speech can get you noticed.
Five great speeches can get you promoted.
Ten great speeches can get you just about
       anywhere you want to go.

May we help you get there?

Sincerely,

Joe Taylor Ford
Editor & Publisher

(Written for the Executive Speechwriter Newsletter
by Joe Taylor Ford. Used with permission of author)

CULTIVATING - Contacting cooled-off hot prospects

Bethel Leadership Institute keeps a record of all inquiries. If a year goes by and the prospects haven't engaged Sheila Murray Bethel for a speech or workshop, they receive this letter.

Dear

In 199__, you asked for information about Sheila Murray Bethel to consider her as a potential speaker at one of your conferences or meetings.

Either Sheila was not chosen or her schedule did not make her available on the dates you requested. In either case, we did not have the pleasure of doing business with you in 199__.

Will you be having any meetings this year where you will be using an outside speaker?

I have enclosed a new brochure about Sheila to remind you about who she is and what she does. If you would like further information, including a video brochure, we will be happy to send it for your consideration.

Sheila's book *Making a Difference* has sold over 80,000 copies and is now out in paperback as well. She has spoken for every type of organization, large and small, in every state plus seventeen foreign countries.

Her speaking schedule fills up quickly, so if you have any interest in Sheila as a potential speaker in the coming year, please let us hold a date for you pending your final decision. Thanks for your interest.

Cordially,

Bill Bethel

CULTIVATING - Contacting cooled-off hot prospects

Dear

Would you like to continue to hear about our [name of product or service]?

If so, please return the enclosed card during the next thirty days, and we'll keep you in our Active File.

By the way, [and here you can give a brief plug such as: "we've just opened a new branch in Oswego," "our newest edition will be on the market in February," "we've added five new styles to our Roanoke line"].

Cordially,

FAMOUS LAST WORDS - WRITE FOR YOUR READER

You now have over a hundred examples of different kinds of sales letters, from cold prospecting to following up on customers. You can adapt and customize these samples to help make your letter writing faster, easier, and more effective.

If you are ever in doubt about how to approach your readers, trade places with them in your imagination and decide what you, the customer, would want to know and how you'd like the information presented for maximum clarity and persuasiveness.

Remember — every letter that goes out over your signature is a potential "sales letter" with the power to promote you, your product, and your company. Make each one count.

INDEX

About the Authors

Eleanor Dugan is the author of more than a dozen books on business writing and communications, including memory, learning, reading, training, problem solving, and selling. Her most recent book is *Rapid Memory*. She is also a film historian.

Bill Bethel is a nationally recognized, award-winning speaker and sales consultant, with more than 3,000 speeches and seminars to his credit. He has been contributing to the bottom lines of his clients and receiving rave reviews for their improved performance for more than 30 years. He has trained and inspired thousands of salespeople to achieve their share of "The American Dream." His most recent book is *Questions That Make the Sale*.